The Dance Steps of Life™

Other Books by Jane Hight McMurry

The Etiquette Advantage®
Readers Theatre for Senior Citizens
Success is a Team Effort

The Dance Steps of Life™

Social Skills That Make A Difference

Jane Hight McMurry

Stellar Publishing

FIRST EDITION 2002
Illustrated by Taylor Desrochers
Book Design by Deb Hobbs

Library of Congress Cataloging-in-Publication Data

McMurry, Jane Hight.
        The Dance Steps of Life/Jane Hight McMurry.
    Includes bibliographical references.
    ISBN 0-9703041-0-2
    1. Etiquette
    2. Social Skills
    3. Interpersonal Communication
    4. Character Development
        I. McMurry, Jane Hight. II. Title.

Library of Congress Control Number: 2001087947

Summary: Explains social skills and manners that facilitate the enjoyment of life.

Printed in the United States of America

Socially Smart™ speaker, author, and trainer Jane Hight McMurry is the president of *Socially Smart*™and founder and managing director of **The Etiquette Advantage**® which provide training and support resources to help people achieve *Socially Smart*™ skills in communicating with people for professional and personal success. She is the author of *The Dance Steps of Life*™, *The Etiquette Advantage*®, *Readers Theatre for Senior Citizens,* and co-author of *Success is a Team Effort.* Jane speaks to audiences at all levels, from the frontline to the boardroom who want to achieve excellence in communicating with people.

PREFACE

Congratulations! The book you're reading will teach you skills that will give you an advantage as you navigate life's social situations. Communication skills are vital to success and The Etiquette Advantage® makes learning these skills fun and interesting. This book is different because it not only uncovers the secrets of what you need to know but also tells many of the stories of why we do what we do. You'll find that knowing these stories makes remembering the skills easy.

I'd like to thank a former student and an organization that asked me to develop a curriculum for use with an underprivileged population for unknowingly starting me on a career path that my family and friends thought had to be a joke. Researching the history of social customs and the challenge of filling a void by creating and developing teaching materials on my subject continues to be an exciting passion.

First, thank you to the former Communication Studies student at the University of North Carolina who said, "This class has really made a difference. I wish I had had a class like this when I was younger." This young man made me think about the importance of positive everyday communication skills as well as the more esoteric communication skills and theories of communication I taught to university students. His comment coupled with the observation of my children and their friends in various situations made me think about how I could further use my subject knowledge, research and teaching skills, and creativity.

Thanks also to The Crossroads Program in Wilmington, NC who asked me to develop a program for underprivileged youth in the community. The focus of that program was not communication, but speech and language – specifically word usage and pronunciation. I observed during the implementation of the curriculum that these children and indeed people from every socio-economic background would likely struggle for success in life no matter how great their language skills, clarity of speech, or degree of math, and science skills unless those basic skills were accompanied by positive social skills.

My search for a curriculum teaching social skills provided leads that I followed. The programs had either no meat in the curriculum or were void of creative instruction. My new career, developing an interesting curriculum to teach social skills, began. I hope that this book, designed as support material to help students remember the skills taught using role-plays, skits, and other interactive strategies, will also be helpful to serendipitous readers interested in what I truly believe are *The Dance Steps of Life* ™.

CONTENTS

INTRODUCTION

Dear Readers,

The Dance Steps of Life™ are not just for kids. The steps are for any person who wants to learn and practice skills that can make a positive difference in life. These skills lead to happiness. How? Bishop Sidney Sanders, a former Episcopal Bishop in North Carolina shared some insight on happiness. He said, if you close your eyes and think about your happiest moment, he could tell you two things about it. "One, you were not thinking about yourself. And two, you were giving or sharing something with someone else."

If the key to happiness is not thinking about yourself, then what is the best way to get over self-consciousness so that you can reach out to others? Being at ease around others arises when an individual can relax and enjoy interpersonal interactions knowing that he possesses the right interpersonal skills for every situation. Life truly is more pleasurable and easier when we know what to expect from other people, what they expect of us, and how to respond in a mannerly way.

All great religions seem to share the best advice regarding how to treat others.

This book cannot improve on that advice. What this book does do is to hone in on the ways North Americans have traditionally liked to be treated. It is my hope that the formal rules, the etiquette, learned in *The Etiquette*

Advantage® programs will increase self-assurance so the participants can reach out to others and make them feel at ease for real happiness comes not from focusing on oneself but from thinking of others. I wish you all the best as you experience the happiness which comes from *The Dance Steps of Life*™.

Jane Hight McMurry

Do as you would be done by.

– Persian

What you would not wish done to yourself, do not do unto others.

– Chinese

Let none of you treat his brother in a way he himself would not like to be treated.

– Mohammedan

The true rule of life is to guard and do by the things of others as they do by their own.

– Hindu

The law imprinted on the hearts of all men is to love the members of society as themselves.

– Roman

One should seek for others the happiness one desires for one's self.

– Buddhist

Do not that to a neighbor which you shall take ill from him.

– Grecian

Do unto others as you would have them do unto you.

– Luke 6:31

The Bishop's Letter

My dear Sisters and Brothers in Christ:

I sit at my desk writing these words looking out on a glorious sun-filled, blue-skyed day. The kind of day that makes even a pessimist like me believe that spring might come, after all. The kind of day that makes me believe that the shoulder that has kept me off the golf course since before Thanksgiving might be getting better. The kind of day that makes me believe that even if Jesus did talk about dividing people into sheep and goats that, in the final analysis, the goats might make it too.

I call on you today to meditate. I call on you to close your eyes and picture that wonderful cartoon drawing of Snoopy, eyes closed, mouth smiling, ears drooping, feet in the air, DANCING. Dancing for the sheer joy of being alive, dancing in ecstasy because of creation.

I call on you for five minutes to stop taking care of things, to stop being clever, important, efficient, imaginative, the perfect career person, wife, mother, father, priest, layperson. Drop it all and let your heart dance.

Let it dance because God created you. Be secure enough in God's love to let it dance because God created you, YOU. As Kathy Mattea sings let this be for you one of those moments when "it seems that all creation is asking us to dance."

Maybe its been so long since you danced that you've forgotten the steps. Not to worry, nobody's watching. Risk it. Close your eyes, droop your ears, feet up in the air, head thrown back. Just for the sheer joy of it and for the love of God; DANCE!

Faithfully,
B. Sidney Sanders
Bishop of East Carolina (deceased)

BODY LANGUAGE

"What you do speaks so loud that I cannot hear what you say."
— *Ralph Waldo Emerson*

Did you know that according to research 93% of our communication is non-verbal and that words account for only 7% of a person's message! Physical appearance contributes to 50% of the first impression and occurs before an individual has spoken. Physical appearance includes every visual aspect including grooming, dress, energy level, and movement. Body language that demonstrates confidence compels people to listen. Facial expression, body posture, position of arms, legs, and feet can convey interest in a conversational partner or reveal anxiety, nervousness, shyness, boredom, or dislike. Effective communicators know spoken words alone are not enough.

Experts agree that people who appear to be the most intelligent and powerful are those who draw the least attention to their hands, legs, feet, and head. The gestures of these people are purposeful.

Unfavorable sitting positions when you are talking to someone include various positions. One of these positions is called the "know it all" position and occurs when crossing one leg over the thigh of the other. A person who sits like this rarely changes his mind especially if he places his hands behind his head. Don't bother trying to bring this person around to your own way of thinking.

Cultural communication problems may also occur when someone sits in this way because in some cultures showing the sole of the foot is considered insulting.

Straddling a chair as if it were a horse is a typically masculine sitting style. Most people typically view this body position unfavorably as it indicates a forceful and domineering manner. Women who sit this way want to be recognized as forceful and dominating.

The study of body language has also shown that the smaller the vocabulary of the speaker the greater the use of gestures. Body language indeed speaks when the brain cannot. Body language is difficult to control but an awareness of what your body can unknowingly communicate is perhaps the only key to its control.

The speaker may look away from the person he is speaking to when he is speaking as part of the normal function of collecting one's thoughts. Direct eye contact is expected 40-60% of the time with the rest of the time letting the eyes roam around the face from the forehead to cheeks to chin. A speaker to several people at one time divides his time between his listeners.

Certain nonverbal patterns can serve as good indicators of a person's true message whether he intends to send the message or not. Experts also agree that to accurately interpret body language, the reader must consider additional environmental clues. The following information is provided to pique your curiosity about body language and to encourage you to consider the messages you are sending with your body as well as what you might discover about your conversational partner.

Meanings of The Most Common Body Language

Arms folded across the chest suggests that the speaker is defensive or in disagreement with the conversational partner. (Note, read body language in clusters of gestures. Crossed arms in a cold environment could simply indicate that the communicator is cold!)

Placing the hands on the hips is interpreted demanding, authoritative, or at least posturing to appear in control.

Legs crossed at the ankle or knee is a positive posture for both men and women indicating that the communicator is relaxed. However, when the communicator swings the crossed leg he appears nervous and ill at ease.

Crossing one leg on top of the other at the thigh thus exposing the sole of the foot makes the communicator appear arrogant and in some cultures is interpreted as rude. This position is known as the "know-it-all" when the arms are clasped behind the head.

Scratching the back of the neck may suggest not only that the communicator may have an itch, but that he is uncertain about something being discussed.

Blinking the eyes ten times or less per minute indicates boredom while fourteen or more blinks shows nervousness and/or stress, or sexual arousal.

Averting the eyes is usually a sure sign of deceit, guilt or lying.

Raised brows coupled with closed eyes for a longer than normal moment sends the message that the communication partner finds something distasteful and surprising.

Ear pulling, eye rubbing, nose rubbing, chin rubbing, and covering the mouth are interpreted by people who read body language to indicate concealment of information, uncertainty, or an untruth being spoken by the communicator. Read body language in gesture clusters and consider the setting and the individual. For example, the person rubbing his eyes and rubbing his nose may be demonstrating an allergic reaction to the cat in the room, not that he is hiding information from someone and cannot look at them. The person covering his mouth may be tired and not intending to convey "I shouldn't say that." The social yawn on the other hand can indicate more than fatigue. Often this person is trying to buy extra time when facing a mildly stressful situation. And finally, even when a person wants to appear to be concentrating on a communicator's message by resting the chin with one hand he is in fact conveying boredom.

Public grooming including rearranging the hair is a reassuring habit that boosts self-confidence. The message to anyone watching is that the person feels good about himself. However, while patting the hair or tossing it back implies that the speaker thinks positively about personal appearance, the habit of a person who twirls strands of hair is indicating confusion, uncertainty and nervousness. Running a hand through the hair generally conveys a sense of being unsure of what to say or do next.

Stroking the Chin is a promising sign that means the listener in interested.

Showing the hands palms up indicates an open and receptive communicator.

Steepling is the gesture of pressing the fingers together and resting the chin or mouth on the fingertips. This gesture indicates deep thought as though the communicator is praying for an answer.

Tugging at the collar is an indicator that the communicator's body temperature has increased. Yes, it might be hot in the room. But the person who knows how to read nonverbal communication is also aware that body temperature increases when people lie. A hand automatically reaching up to let air in by loosening the collar is truly demonstrating that a person is hot under the collar.

Stroking the necktie is a nonverbal signal that the communicator is trying hard to please and is desirous of making a good impression.

Shoving hands into a shirt, blouse, jacket or pocket is thought to signal that the communicator is secretive and may not want to communicate. After all, hands thrust deep into the pockets are not available for shaking hands or for any other form of tactile communication. Preoccupation with money (either too much or not enough) is another interpretation when the hand in the pocket jingles money.

Jiggling the foot back and forth when the legs are crossed, tapping the foot on the floor and drumming the fingers on the dining table indicate an attempt by the body to run from the setting...parts of the body are already running away! This communicator is very likely nervous or bored.

Fidgeting with shirt cuffs or jewelry on the wrists signals a need for attention.

Holding hands or objects in front of the body such as a book or magazine indicates an anxious person desiring a communication barrier. Pulling objects from a briefcase or purse when entering a room gives the message that the person is not prepared and/or stalling for time.

Spreading out when sitting sends off unfavorable messages for both men and women, though the unfavorable message is different for each sex. The man who sits spreading out is signaling that he is taking over, while men interpret a woman who is spreading out as overstepping her bounds. However, if she places only one arm on a nearby chair the nonverbal message is that she wants to be perceived as having equal authority.

Making Conversation Points Using the Hands

The hands can be quite effective in communicating ideas. Pointing a finger at any one in any culture is likely to generate bad feelings. However, the fingers can be used effectively to reinforce communication that contains numerous items.

Conversation that includes several points can be made easier to follow by using the fingers. Try to keep oral lists to three items as more than three increases the difficulty of oral comprehension. North Americans begin the count with the index finger, followed by the middle finger and ring finger. Europeans typically begin the count with the thumb followed by the index finger and middle finger.

Body Language

The less you rely on gestures, the more authoritative and confident you'll appear. Work on developing your vocabulary so you'll rely less on gestures. Stand with your hands by your side or clasped behind your back. (To perfectly align your body, clasp your hands behind your back and release hands by your side. Clasping your hands behind your back pulls your shoulder blades back and down. Keep your chin parallel to the floor.)

Habits to Avoid

- Keep hands out of pockets.

- Avoid nervous habits such as biting nails, cracking knuckles and twisting hair.

- Avoid chewing gum in public.

- Avoid using verbal phrases which are over used such as like, you know, like I said, you know, and uh, and umm.

"We could learn a lot from crayons: some are sharp, some are pretty, some are dull, some have weird names, and all are different colors...but they all have to learn to live in the same box."

Unknown

GOOD GROOMING

You demonstrate respect for yourself and others by the way you present yourself. Good grooming shows that you care about your appearance and that you are concerned about making a good impression. Most importantly it shows that you care about the comfort of others.

Grooming Basics
- Grooming basics begin with a daily bath or shower.
- Rinse all soap from your body and all shampoo from your hair.
- Use a nailbrush on finger nails, elbows, toes and heels.
- Dry thoroughly and use a light lotion to prevent dryness.

Clean, Shiny Hair
- Wash your hair when needed. Some people need to shampoo their hair every day; those with very dry hair may be able to wash their hair only a few times a week.
- Use a wide-tooth comb and start at the bottom when combing wet hair.

Dental Details
- Brush and floss your teeth properly at least twice a day.
- Ask your dentist to demonstrate correct brushing if you feel you aren't brushing properly.
- Brush your teeth before bed.
- If the bristles of your toothbrush are worn out or splayed, you are brushing too roughly.

- Brush gently—gum damage can occur if you scrub too hard.
- Brush in a gentle, circular motion, one tooth at a time.
- Lightly brush your tongue.

Fingernails

Both men and women need to take care of their fingernails. Your nail supplies should include: nail file or emery board, polish remover, clippers, cotton balls, cuticle removing cream, white manicure pencil and sharpener, buffing stick, and nail polish.

WALKING IN PUBLIC

Women do not link arms with men when walking in public unless they are old or infirm. At night, a woman may link arms with the man by placing the palm of her hand lightly within the curve of the man's elbow. (See escort position on page 117.)

The man always walks nearest the curb unless the side away from the curb is very crowded. This tradition began long ago when men walked on the side closest to the road to protect women from the splashes made by horses and carriages in unpaved streets. In addition, it was an early custom in an area called The Shambles in York, England for people to throw their garbage out of the second floor windows. The upper stories of the buildings along The Shambles tipped towards the street so it was much safer for women to walk close to the lower level of the buildings where they were less likely to be hit with falling trash!

A man escorting two women does not sandwich himself between them, but takes his place nearest the street's curb. The older of the two women stands in the middle and the younger woman walks by the older woman's side. Although unpaved roads and mudsplaying horses are rare and waste disposal laws are enforced, the custom of men walking curbside is still practiced by courteous men.

Situations When It Is Courteous For The Man To Walk Ahead of a Woman

- A man should go first whenever not doing so will cause confusion. A man precedes a woman through crowds, staying slightly ahead of th ewoman so she can easily follow.

- A man precedes a woman when walking through a train so he can open and close the succession of heavy doors.

- A man precedes a woman into a taxi, but first tells her that he will get in first so she won't have to slide over. When the woman has entered the taxi he reaches over and closes the door. A man gets out of a taxi, subway, train, or bus first so he can assist the woman out. He exits a limo first, unless there is doorman.

- Men open doors for women. The man walks ahead of a woman and pulls the door open and then steps back allowing the woman to walk first through the door. If the door is hung so that it pushes forward, the man walks through the door first pushing the door forward and holding the door for the woman. When the door does not automatically revolve, the man steps ahead of the woman and pushes the door to get it moving. On elevators, whoever is closest to the door should get on and off first.

- A man leads the way when looking for seats at events including the theatre and church unless there is an usher. At church, he stands in the aisle with his back to the altar and lets the woman enter first.

- A man climbs in and out of a small boat first (unless it sinking) so he can help a woman up or down the ramp.

- A man precedes the woman down stairs and escalators to break possible falls and he goes up escalators and stairs before her to ensure her modesty.

- He leads the way to the table in a restaurant unless a restaurant employee leads the way.

- A man precedes a woman onto the dance floor.

PERSONAL HABITS

Acceptable personal habits vary from nation to nation. Behavior that is polite in one country may be considered rude in other lands. For example, burping after a meal is a sign of satisfaction and is encouraged after a meal in some areas. In the United States it is considered impolite to burp in public. The old saying, "When in Rome do as the Romans do" may be followed. Learn the customs and traditions of the people you visit.

In the United States of America, do as polite Americans do:

- AVOID burping

- AVOID cleaning your ears in public

- AVOID picking your nose in public

- AVOID picking your teeth in public

- AVOID talking about the cost of your or others belongings

- AVOID telling secrets in front of others

- AVOID scratching in public

- AVOID smacking and popping gum in public

- AVOID spitting-unless it is necessary (for example, if you discover a foreign object in the food you are chewing)

- AVOID swearing

- ALWAYS cover your mouth when coughing or sneezing

- ALWAYS use a handkerchief or Kleenex when you blow your nose

- ALWAYS excuse yourself from the table when experiencing a coughing or sneezing attack

- ALWAYS flush the toilet

- Men ALWAYS lower the toilet seat after using the toilet

CHEWING GUM AND MINTS

Chewing gum and mints taste great. Best of all you can blow big bubbles with fat wads of gum! The worst part of gum is that it can be very annoying to the people around you. Gum chewing etiquette is simple--just think about the feelings of those around you before you smack, blow and pop. Most mints refresh the breath and don't require the sight and sound effects of gum. The tips below will guide you as you choose the time and place to enjoy gum and mints.

Chew gum and mints that require chewing in places where the smacking noise of gum and the continual movement of the mouth and jaw won't distract or bother other people. Enjoy chewing gum when your friends or family offer it to you and are chewing it or any time you're alone. Remove your chewing gum when using the telephone as chewing sounds are transmitted. Place used gum in a piece of paper and throw it into a trash can where it won't create a gooey mess. It is acceptable to say no thank you when offered chewing gum. The offer of a breath mint may be a hint so breath mints usually should be accepted.

Follow these simple chewing gum rules:

• Never let chewing gum be seen.

• Gum should never be heard.

- Dispose of chewed gum permanently. The street, sidewalk, behind the ear, or under the table or dinner plate is not acceptable.

- Never take a stick of gum for yourself and not offer one to others. Offer half of a stick of gum if you have only one or wait until you are alone if several people are present.

Places to avoid chewing include:

- Classrooms where listening and concentration are necessary,

- Places of worship that are deemed holy,

- Theatres and musical events where people are listening, and

- Museums and libraries where silence is requested and valuable objects may be ruined by gum that might unexpectedly pop out of the mouth.

HELPFUL HINT: Peanut butter will remove ABC (already been chewed) gum from hair and skin.

MAGIC WORDS

The words we choose to use can help us get what we want and help people have a good feeling when they are around us. Use the following words often and you'll see doors open to you as if by magic!

* Thank-you

* Please

* May I?

* Excuse me

* Pardon me

* I'm sorry

* After you

* You first

* Your choice

* You choose

* Great job

* Good going

* I need your help

* You're a big help

* You're great, smart, fun

* Great idea

* Good thinking

* Congratulations

"Good habits are not made on birthdays, nor at the New Year. The workshop of character is everyday life."

Malthie D. Babcock

HANDSHAKING

Handshaking is the accepted greeting in the United States for men and women in almost every country around the world. Even the Japanese will bow and shake hands when beginning and ending a meeting in the Western world. The modern custom in the USA is for both men and women to shake hands. (The old custom of a man waiting for a woman to extend her hand first is out of date although some older men and women adhere to this old social rule.) (Exception: In European countries, the woman offers her hand first.) Don't hold back—extend your hand immediately. You are judged by your handshake. A warm, sincere handshake makes a positive, tactile connection with another person.

Always be ready to initiate and receive a handshake.

Stand up when shaking hands to show respect for yourself and for others. Notice that in the photo on the left the woman is not standing. She is practicing social etiquette, which is still in use in some areas of the United States and is certainly correct. However, you might be interested to know that the history for this custom is based on the antiquated notion that females were once considered weaker than males. Women did not fully participate in the activities they do now.

The modern tradition abandons the notion of weakness so women who want to be treated equally — especially if they want to participate fully in American life stand and shake hands for introductions. The man in the photo on the left should also stand for the introduction. Stand an arm's length from people when conversing.

All stand for introductions

How to Shake Hands

1. Extend your hand vertically with the thumb up and out to the person opposite you. (Avoid curving your hand or offering only your fingertips.)

2. Connect the web of your hand firmly to the web of the other person.

3. Keep your hand firm with some tension. No one likes the "limp fish" handshake! (Don't squeeze too hard.)

4. Shake from the elbow not the wrist or shoulder.

5. Pump the person's hand smoothly for two to three pumps.

6. Look the person in the eye, smile, and lean slightly forward.

When to Shake Hands

- Shake hands with your host first.

- Shake hands during introductions.

- Shake when saying hello or good-bye.

- In the United States, a handshake is often used between people making a deal. The pledging of words between people who trust each other is valued more than many written contracts between people who distrust each other.

- Shake when congratulating someone or when extending sympathy.

- Shake hands with someone who comes to your home and when bidding farewell.

- Shake hands when entering or leaving a room.

Negative Handshakes

The Bone Crusher. This person is seen as aggressive, angry and intimidating.

The Fingertip Extender. Many women were taught to offer their fingertips only. This is a weak, unsatisfying handshake.

The Limp Fish. A handshake with no tension or tone in the hand. The shake feels weak and lifeless.

The Gloved Handshake. Sometimes referred to as the "preacher" handshake, this handshake conveys the message of comfort and consolation. The gloved handshake occurs when the person giving the shake places his left hand on top of the person's hand he is clasping with his right hand. It is best used with close friends or when conveying sympathy or offering comfort. The gloved handshake should not be used as an everyday greeting.

Handshaking Hindrances

- Carry a handkerchief or small powder puff in your pocket if you are prone to clammy or perspiring hands. Squeeze it to discreetly absorb perspiration. Or use antiperspirant on your hands 24 hours before an event. A product called drysol is available by prescription. If your problem is severe, ask your physician to prescribe drysol for you.

- Remember to wipe your hands off before shaking someone's hand if your hands are dirty. If not, simply say "I'd like to shake hands, but I have 'spaghetti sauce' on them."

- Rings can be painful when shaking hands—it's best not to wear them on the right hand.

- Older women were taught they should extend their hand first. This traditional social etiquette is changing in today's world. (In European countries, the woman still offers her hand first.) Today it doesn't matter who offers a hand first, however, no one should refuse or ignore an outstretched hand.

How to Handle Disabilities and Handshaking

It is appropriate to shake hands or touch a person who has a disability. Remember that a person with a disability does not have a contagious disease and should never be pre-judged or defined by his disabiliy. The impression you make will be positive as physically challenged individuals appreciate the same gestures of courtesy and respect extended to anyone else. Treat physically challenged people with the same respect, courtesy, and consideration you appreciate.

- If the person has an artificial limb, it's okay to touch his upper arm or the prosthesis in greeting.

- The physically challenged person who has a prosthetic right hand may extend his left hand. Senator Robert Dole shakes with his left hand because his right one is withered from a combat injury.

- Paralyzed people appreciate being recognized too with a handshake. Squeeze their arm or hand.

- When greeting a blind person you may say, "I'd like to shake your hand" then wait for the person to offer his hand.

- Speak directly to the physically challengedrather than through a thrid person.

- Be thoughtful of the extra time it might take for a physically challenged person to move or to complete a task.

"The measure of a man's real character is what he would do if he knew he would never be found out."

Thomas Macaulay

HOW TO STAND AND HOW TO SIT

Standing straight and tall will make you appear more confident. You will look thinner and your clothes will hang better. In Victorian times young women were made to sit on a stool with a board strapped to their backs to help them develop perfect posture! Many people practice perfect posture by walking while balancing a book on top of their heads. Other ways you can practice include pretending to be a puppet—standing perfectly straight as though someone were pulling you up with a string from the top of your head. Or, clasping your hands behind you and then allowing your hands to fall to your sides. Your shoulders should be back and down and your chin parallel to the floor. Tuck your buttocks in and suck in your stomach slightly.

The best standing position is with hands out of the pockets relaxed and by your side. The second best standing position is to clasp the hands behind your back.

Avoid the fig-leaf standing position that makes you appear less open to communicate with others.

How to Sit and Rise from a Seated Position

- Approach the chair.

- Turn, find the chair with the back of the leg.

- Sit on the edge of the chair and scoot the buttocks back, sitting erect.

- Choose a more rigid chair when possible. It's difficult to look graceful when enveloped by an overstuffed or oversized piece of furniture.

- Slide forward when rising, pause and stand gracefully. Don't leap out of the chair.

- Place your feet properly. Men and women may both sit with their feet flat on the floor, or the woman may cross her ankles. Be aware of the cultural differences when conducting business internationally. The sole of the foot is considered offensive in Saudi Arabia and Asian cultures so the legs are never crossed with the ankle resting on the knee, exposing the sole of the foot.

The man in the photo to the left has his legs spread apart which gives him the appearance of total relaxation and not someone ready to take an active part in conversation. His buttoned jacket looks like it is about to pop.

The man in the photo at the right also appears relaxed. This is a common sitting position for some groups of American men. However, as discussed earlier, this body language is generally considered negative.

Strive for variations of the following neutral sitting positions.

Below are three variations of a good sitting position for women. The drawback of the sitting position of the woman in the far right picture is the tendency to shake the leg which will make her appear nervous. Men may also choose to sit with one leg crossed over the other.

Positive, open, relaxed body language

Rise from your seat by sliding forward in your chair, pausing slightly, and standing gracefully.

"People will forget what you said,
people will forget what you did,
but people will never forget
how you made them feel."

Unknown

WHEN TO STAND

All Stand For Introductions

Modern manners encourage everyone to stand for introductions. Standing to meet someone is a gesture of self-respect and respect to those in attendance.

Note to women: In earlier days, older women did not stand when a man or younger woman was presented. Today, modern women do stand unless a physical limitation may prevent it or make the motion awkward. In addition, women did not shake hands with all they met. Today, women correctly shake hands with persons of any age as a sign of respect.

The seated woman in the photo is practicing traditional social etiquette.

Host and Hostess Stand

Stand to greet all guests.

Family Members Stand

All family members stand when a guest enters a room in their home. Every member of the host's family should rise when a guest enters the room as well as greet the guests with a pleasant greeting, a welcoming smile, firm handshake, and good eye contact. A child sitting and already talking with an adult guest need not rise each time a guest comes into the room unless the guest is brought to him/her for an introduction. In that case, all rise for introductions.

Men Stand

A man stands when a woman enters the room for the first time and continues to stand until the woman is seated or leaves the area.

A man stands when a woman comes to sit by him. The man sits after the woman is seated. A man stands when a woman leaves.

Note: The man stands for every woman who enters his area and stops to talk. He does not need to rise for unknown women who are simply passing through his area. A man makes the gesture of half-rising and nodding when a woman passes his table when he is dining. The man completely stands if the woman stops to talk. He does not sit until the woman sits or leaves.

Both men should stand as a sign of respect when they greet others.

"The manner of others towards us is usually the reflex of our manner towards them. As men have howled into the wood so it has ever howled out."

Alfred Ayres, 1884,
The Mentor

INTRODUCTIONS

Meeting and Greeting includes smiling, making eye contact, saying hello, and standing up to shake hands by both women and men. In the olden days, a woman stood only to meet and greet an older woman or dignitary. Further, a woman did not shake hands unless she chose to extend her hand to a man. Today, equal respect is shown to both sexes. The most important part of meeting and greeting is called the *introduction.*

Introductions are the way we make ourselves or our family and friends known to others. We've all been in that awkward situation when we encounter a friend who is with someone we don't know. We talk for a moment and the unknown person stands there uncomfortably. No move is made to introduce the stranger. We leave the encounter feeling unfulfilled and a bit guilty. The stranger leaves the encounter feeling unfulfilled and angry. The outward appearance is that he wasn't important enough to be acknowledged. The real reason is that his friend neglected to make the introduction because he felt insecure about how to do so.

How to Introduce Yourself

- Stand up, look the person in the eye, and extend your hand for a firm web to web handshake and say your name and something about yourself. For example, "Hello, I'm Jane McMurry. I'm Kathy's tennis partner from Wilmington."

- The key is to give as much concise information about yourself as possible in a short amount of time. This is conversation bait.

- Conversation bait encourages the other person to respond to the information.
  "It's nice to meet you. I'm Jane's friend, Ronna Zimmer, who went with the tennis group to Camp Cathy last summer."

How to Properly Introduce Others

- Stand up and make eye contact as you are saying each person's name.

- Say the older, more important, or female's name first followed by one of the following phrases: "I'd like to present to you," "I would like to introduce to you," "I would like for you to meet," or simply, "this is" followed by the name of the person being introduced. For example, "Becky Jones, I'd like to introduce to you my sister, Judy Fulk."

- Make each person feel important by providing important information about each person as you make the introduction. Telling about the interests, special talents, home towns or even the schools of the people being introduced will give a basis for small talk. For example, say, "Winston, I'd like to introduce you to my friend from camp, Jeremiah, who is a magician from Montreal, Canada." An introduction such as this can result in several avenues of conversation - camp experience, magic, the city of Montreal and the country of Canada!

Important!

If you come upon a friend and a group of people you don't know, make the first move—introduce yourself!

Three Rules for Making Proper Social Introductions

Introduce:

- Less important persons to more important persons
- Men to women
- Younger people to older people (Accomplish this by saying the more important woman's, or older person's name first)

Exceptions

- When introducing another person and a family member, the other person is given precedence—except when as a child you are introducing your mother or father.

- Women are presented to ambassadors, chiefs of state, royalty and dignitaries of the church.

Polish your introductions by practicing the following:

- Introduce a less important person to a more important person if you can determine the more important person. Do this by first saying the more important person's name. For example, "Mr. President, I'd like to present to you my uncle, Governor Nutting." Or Professor Stamey, I'd like to introduce to you my roommate from Virginia, Karen Layman."

- Introduce a man to a woman when they are the same age. Do this by first saying the woman's name.

Examples
"Ellen Carter, I'd like to introduce to you my neighbor, Howard Allen." "Howard, Ellen is my good friend from Wilmington."

- Introduce a younger person to an older person. Do this by first saying the older person's name. For example, say, "Grandmother, I'd like to introduce to you my guitar teacher Ms. Poole. Ms. Poole, this is my grandmother, Joan Hight, from Henderson."

- Introduce a new friend to a group. Do this by first saying the new friend's name. For example, say, "Dale Zimmer, I'd like you to meet my friends." Then say the names of the members in the group or have your friends introduce themselves to your friend.

Example of Introducing a Parent and a Friend
"Mom, I'd like to introduce to you my friend, Eleanor Wilkins. Eleanor, this is my mom, Mrs. Hight who made the homemade cookies for our trip to the coast."
"Dad, I'd like to introduce to you my friend, Pat Koonce who was in Gene's class at Dartmouth. Pat, this is my father, Mr. Hight."

Examples of Introductions to Church and Government Officials
"Bishop Daniels, I'd like to introduce to you my friend, Mary Arthur Stoudemire. She serves on the vestry at The Chapel of the Cross in Chapel Hill. "
"Mr. President, may I present Worth Price, the Vice President at Allied Pharmaceutical."

Example of Introducing Your Teacher and a Parent
(Even if your teacher is younger than your parents, show deference and respect to her by making her the most important person in the way you phrase the introduction.)

"Ms. Barry, I'd like to introduce to you my mother, Joan Hight. Mom, this is my math teacher Ms. Barry."

Example of Family Introductions
"Beth Marshall, I'd like to introduce my brother, Chip Hight who is a Superior Court Judge in the 9th judicial district. Chip, Beth practices civil law in Winston-Salem."

Example of Introducing Two Friends to Each Other
"Wendy Murphy, I'd like to introduce Terri Haywood. Wendy, I met Terri this summer at the Outing Club. Terri, Wendy is the friend I told you about who has the house on the mountain lake in New Hampshire." (Provide something of interest to talk about.)

Rise for Introductions

Always rise for any introduction. Rising is a gesture of respect for both the person to whom you are being introduced and yourself.

Handling Honorifics

An honorific is a title such as Miss, Ms., Mrs., Reverend, and Dr.

• Use an honorific when addressing an adult. This not only demonstrates respect for the adult, but also clues the other person that the adult should be addressed using the stated honorific. For example, it would be incorrect for a young person to say, "Clayton, I'd like to introduce to you my classmate, Elizabeth Miars." Instead, the young person should say, " Dr. Callaway, I'd like to introduce my classmate Elizabeth Miars."

- When someone has a title, use it correctly. Greet your doctor or dentist by saying "Hello, Dr. Craig." NOT "Hi, Mr. Craig."

Responding to Introductions

- Do not reply with a simple "Hi," or "Hello."

- Stand up, extend your hand, smile, lean toward the person and say, "Hello, David. How do you do." Some people prefer to say the phrase "It's nice to meet you." However, the traditional response is "How do you do."

- Repeat the person's name.

- Ask the person to repeat the name if you didn't hear the name properly or are unsure of how to pronounce it.

RESPECT FOR THOSE WE LIVE WITH

Respect means…"always showing consideration."

Living with family members or roommates every single day can be a fun happy experience or it can be a nightmare. The good thing about living with others is that we are comfortable with them because they know us well. However, unless we are careful to respect those we live with, and they are careful to respect us, the otherwise happy home life can quickly erode and leave everyone unhappy. Sometimes we annoy others and do not even know what we have done. Let's take a look at what we can do to make our living arrangements happy.

Treat Those You Live With The Way You Want To Be Treated

Notice what is going on in your environment and consider what you can do to make the environment pleasant for those you share it with. For example, if someone is napping, studying, or talking on the telephone be quiet. Don't listen in to others telephone conversations or interrupt others when they are talking.

Respect Authority

Don't argue or talk back. If you disagree, learn to express yourself politely.

Respect the Feelings of Those with Whom You Live

Brothers and sisters can fight one minute and be best friends the next. If you and your siblings don't have a great relationship, think about developing a plan to get along better. You won't always be best friends, but you must have respect for one another.

Respect the Property of Others

If you want to borrow something, ask. Return whatever you borrow as soon as you finish with it and return it in as good or better condition as when you borrowed it. If you break something, confess. Knock on closed doors before you enter. Do not open the mail of others.

Share Your Belongings with Others

Take Care of Your Room and Your Belongings
Parents work hard to provide shelter, clothes and toys for their children. Show appreciation by caring for your possessions appropriately.

Put Back Everything You Take Out

Contribute to the Care of Your Home and Your Yard
Practice good kitchen etiquette. Help in the kitchen by helping to set the table, wash dishes, and sweep. Follow good bathroom etiquette. Help around the house by straightening up. Take out the trash. Rake the leaves, and weed the garden. Do these things without being asked.

Clean Up Every Mess You Make

Keep the Business of Those You Live with Private
Don't share information about those you live with if someone is having difficulty at school or at work. Keep the finances of those you live with private.

Say "Please" and "Thank you" to Those with Whom You Live

"A rising tide lifts all boats."

American Saying,1960s,
Popularized by the Kennedy Family

RESPECT FOR PEOPLE AT SCHOOL

School is where you spend most of your time. Obviously you want to have fun, make friends and learn.

Three phrases should be part of your vocabulary at school or anywhere you go: "Please," "May I," "Thank you!"

Here are some tips to help you get along with others and be well-liked and well-respected:

Respect for Teachers

1. As you enter the classroom each day, greet your teacher. Avoid just a mumbling, "Hi," Say, "Good morning, Ms. Goodrum!" enthusiastically and with a smile. Teachers are people, too—they like to be acknowledged and respected.

2. Follow the teacher's instructions.

3. Show respect by not talking when the teacher is speaking. Students who follow the rules help the teacher run the class in a peaceful manner.

4. Don't argue with the teacher or talk back—the ultimate sign of disrespect. Having another opinion or questioning is okay—learn to express yourself politely.

5. If others are making trouble, don't join in. Never make fun of a teacher or anyone in authority behind his back.

Question: Which Students do Teachers Like?

Answer: Teachers Like Students Who

… Pay attention.

… Are patient and wait their turn.

… Remember to raise their hands and are recognized before speaking.

… Are responsible for their possessions including books.

… Do their homework on time.

… Are active in classroom discussions.

Question: Which Students do Teachers Dislike?

Answer: Teachers Dislike Students Who

… Interrupt them when they are teaching.

… Do not raise their hands to ask questions.

...Do not pay attention and talk to their classmates at inappropriate times.

... Chew gum in class.

... Write on their desks and deface school property.

... Cheat.

... Break in line and do not take turns.

Respect for Classmates – Kindness is Key

1. As you take your seat each day, greet your classmates. Put a smile on your face. Everyone likes someone who is cheerful and friendly.

2. Show interest in those around you. Know the names of the people who sit next to you. Even if they aren't your best friends, be friendly and smile. Widen your circle of friends and acquaintances.

3. If someone looks sad or lonely, make the first move. Introduce yourself, ask if they need help or have a question. Show your kindness.

4. Participate and cooperate. You might not think every game or every activity is fun, but participate anyway—you might be surprised! Teachers and friends appreciate students and friends who are willing to try new things with an open attitude.

Good Manners in the Cafeteria

- Avoid Really Loud Talking

- Wait Your Turn in Line – Never Push!

- Clean Up after You Eat

- Never Throw Food

Good Manners in the Computer Lab

- Work Quietly

- Help Others Whenever Possible

- Keep the Computer Area Neat

- Treat the Computers with Respect – Never Hit the Machines!

- Be Careful Not to Drink Around the Computers – Spilled Beverages Can Ruin Computers

- Never Open Files Which are Not Yours

Good Manners on the Playground

- Include Everyone Who Wants to Play

- Be Careful With Sports Equipment

- Don't Fight

- Never Hurt People by Calling Names

Good Manners in the Library

- Whisper if You Must Talk

- Return Books When You are Finished

- Do Not Eat or Drink

- Keep Your Work Area Tidy

Good Manners in the Halls

- Walk Quietly

- Pick Up Trash You Find in the Hall

- Avoid Looking into Other Classrooms

"Reputation is what you are supposed to be;
Character is what you are.
Reputation is made in a moment;
Character is built in a lifetime."

William H. Davis

BUS ETIQUETTE

School buses and public buses are exciting forms of transportation. We can sit with all of our friends and travel to school, around town, or to events at a distance from where we live. However, courtesy is important for the enjoyment of everyone on the bus as well as to ensure the safety of all passengers.

Tips for Riding on a Bus

- Wait your turn to board the bus. Do not push or break in line.

- Offer assistance to passengers who need it. Lending a hand with heavy bags is appreciated.

- Say "Hello," and "Good-bye" to the driver.

- Take your seat on the bus and remain seated. It is dangerous to walk around when the bus is moving.

- Offer your seat to people less fit including pregnant women and the elderly.

- Talk in a normal voice to friends on the bus. Yelling and screaming on the bus is distracting to the driver and could cause the driver to have an accident.

- Avoid talking on cell phones on the bus. Conversations in confined areas can be heard by others and are annoying.

- Respect fellow passengers by listening to your radio or boom box with a headset. Taste in music varies.

- Keep your possessions with you and out of the way of other passengers.

- Remove all of your possessions including your trash when you exit the bus.

KITCHEN ETIQUETTE

Always wash your hands with soap before cooking, eating or making yourself a drink or snack.

Don't leave your dishes on the table, the counter or in the sink. Rinse them and put them in the dishwasher. Put detergent in and start the dishwasher when it is full. If it is filled with clean dishes, empty the dishwasher and then load your dirty dishes.

Wipe the counter and around the sink when you are finished. Pick up the ice cubes you drop on the floor. If you spill something in the refrigerator, wipe up the mess.

Tell the grocery shopper in your home when you use the last of something, or write it on a list. In addition, if you finish a box or carton of something, throw the empty container or wrapping away.

If you see something unusual or interesting in the refrigerator, ask before you begin snacking. Those may be the ingredients for something special.

Refill the ice cube trays after taking a few cubes. Don't just put the empty trays back in the freezer.

"One hand washes the other; give and take."

Epicharmus (530-440 B.C.)

BATHROOM ETIQUETTE

If you use the last of the shampoo, toothpaste, or toilet paper, let the family grocery shopper know. If you use the last of the toilet paper, put another roll on the dispenser.

Wipe the drops of water from around the sink after you wash your hands.

Rinse the bowl of the sink after you brush your teeth.

Flush the toilet and close the toilet lid after you use it.

Wipe the hair off the floor after you brush your hair. Clean the hair from the drain after you shower or bathe.

Fold your towel neatly and hang it up after you use it. Do not refold a guest towel so that someone else will mistake it for unused. Avoid using the host's personal towels unless no guest towels have been left out for you and you have no other towels to use.

Attendants in public bathrooms should be tipped fifty cents or more if they provide some special services.

"Clothes make the man. Naked people have little or no influence in society."

Mark Twain

COAT ETIQUETTE

Thoughtfulness of others is the root of all manners. In long ago times when women wore wide bustling gowns in drafty castles, venturing out of doors could be either a cold or cumbersome affair without the aid of some masculine chivalry. Knights or pages would help the ladies don their capes. Today, men still assist women with coats, but it is also kind and polite for a woman to help a man with his coat if he needs assistance.

Helping to Put on Coats

Hold the coat at the shoulders so that the coat is low enough for the wearer to put his/her right arm in first. Continue holding the coat while the wearer inserts the left arm into the left coat sleeve. Do not let go of the coat until the wearer has it on securely. This kind act will avoid having the coat fall to the floor.

Helping to Remove a Coat

The helper stands behind the person and holds the coat at the shoulders, slowly lowering the coat until it is removed. The person helping to remove the coat should then take the coat to the closet and hang it up or check the coat at the coat check station.

Coat Checks

Check rooms are often available in theatres and restaurants. This thoughtful service is easy to use. Give your coats or bulky packages to the attendant who will in turn give you a ticket bearing the number of your coat hanger or packages. Wait your turn in line to collect your items from the coat check and then present your checkroom ticket and pay a small service fee if required. If a fee is not required, it is expected that a tip of fifty cents to a dollar per checked item be given. In the unfortunate event that you lose your ticket claim, you must describe your belongings in detail to the attendant. Consider people waiting in line and allow them to go ahead of you when retrieval of your items requires extra time.

• Always thank your host and say goodbye before you get your coat. Avoid saying goodbye to your host with your coat over your arm as this is just as bad manners as saying goodbye to your host after you've put on your coat.

COATS AND CRAVATS

Men's clothing has evolved from loin clothes and knightly suits of mail to tennis togs and three piece straight jackets! Clothing choices then and now provide a means of identifying friends and enemies by noting clothing styles and details of dress. The tartan's plaid signals a certain Scottish clan, a uniform's color identifies a soldier's country and a shoe's type indicates a wearer's activity preference be it soccer, tennis or formal affair.

Today's wearer offers personality clues to the modern observer much the same as in yesteryear. Clothing traditionally worn by either a woman or a man is now acceptable for both sexes to wear. Nevertheless, while many moderns throw customs and traditions to the wind, others note minute details of dress to learn about the wearer. The fabric of a frock and the width of a necktie's knot have all been known to offer clues to serious inspectors like Sherlock Holmes and James Bond. 007 detected a Russian spy who was impersonating an upper class English gentleman because the spy's necktie knot was wide and not the slim necktie knot worn by British aristocrats!

Cravats

Croatian soldiers in the 18th century were the first to wear neckties. King Louis XIV liked the look, adapted it, wore it and called it a "cravat." Royalty set this fashion which is worn now by men and women. Today the English call it a cravat, Americans simply call it a tie.

Coats

Royalty set another fashion regarding the buttoning and unbuttoning of coats. All royalty kept their coats fastened when standing and sitting until the reign of portly Edward VII of England who was affectionately known as Bertie. Big Bertie's' buttons bulged at certain times so he unfastened them out of necessity. Those around him observed and copied. Keen observers could distinguish people who were often in the King's presence from those who were not. Here's what Bertie did and what is still in practice today:

- On a two-button single-breasted jacket only the top button is buttoned when standing. Unbutton when sitting.

- On a three-button jacket the middle button is buttoned when standing. Unbutton when sitting.

- On a double-breasted jacket the lower two buttons are buttoned when standing, the lowest is unbuttoned when sitting.

- On a vest the lowest button is not fastened.

- The shirt cuff shows half an inch below the jacket sleeve.

- The jacket covers the seat of the trousers.

- The trousers break on the shoes in front and are slightly longer at the back when standing.

HOW TO TIE A NECKTIE

Well-dressed gentlemen know how to tie bow and neckties correctly. Follow these simple diagrams and you'll quickly master techniques for tying a tie.

How to Tie a Bow Tie

- Start with one end about one and one-half inches below the other and bring the long end through the center.

- Form a loop with the short end and center it where the knot will be.

- Bring the long end over it.

- Form a loop with the long end and push it through the knot behind the front loop.

- Adjust the ends slowly so that they are about the same on either side of the knot.

How to Tie a Half Windsor Knot

- Place the tie around your neck with the wider end hanging on the right side of your chest about twelve inches below the narrow end which is hanging over the left side of your chest.

- Cross the wide end over the narrow end and pull it around and underneath the narrow end.

- Carry the wide end up through the loop and pass it around the front from left to right.

- Bring the wide end through the loop again and pass it through the knot in front.

- Tighten the knot slowly as you draw it up to the collar.

How to Tie a Four-in Hand Knot

- Place the tie around your neck with the wider end hanging on the right side of your chest about twelve inches below the narrow end which is hanging over the left side of your chest.

- Cross the wide end over the narrow end and pull it up through the loop.

- Hold the front of the knot loosely with the index finger and pull the wide end through the loop in front.

- Tighten the knot slowly while holding the narrow end and sliding the knot to the collar.

"Fine feathers do not always make fine birds."

Richard Wells,1890,
Manners, Customs, and Dress

HAT ETIQUETTE

Chivalrous knights of the Middle Ages wore full armor in public. Knights raised helmet visors as a sign of mutual recognition. The knight removed his helmet entirely when in the company of friends. The complete removal of his helmet symbolized his belief that he was safe among friends and without need of his protecting helmet.

Today's knightly gentleman:

- Raises his hat in recognition of a friend when passing and removes his hat completely in the presence of an assembly of friends.

- Removes his hat with his left hand leaving his right hand free to shake hands - or removes with right and transfers to the left hand.

- Tips his hat to a woman and removes it completely when speaking to her. He may replace his hat if he and the woman walk ahead together.

- Removes his hat inside all buildings.

- Removes his hat when he says the pledge of allegiance and when the American flag passes in a parade.

Ladies of yore often wore jeweled wigs and elaborate hats. Removal of their hats could have jolted a fine wig's precarious position. Thus, a well-bred woman never removed her hat when inside or outside of buildings. The same holds true today, except thoughtfulness of others - our standard of courtesy today - requires that a lady remove her hat in situations where a hat might obstruct another's view.

GLOVE ETIQUETTE

The custom of wearing gloves is very old. In Egyptian hieroglyphics, the glove symbolizes the hand. Gloves originally were worn for protection from cold weather and from the danger of battle. In the Middle Ages, women began to wear gloves for fashion.

Today people still wear gloves for protection and fashion. The custom of when to leave on gloves and when to remove them hinges on the past.

Knights removed their gauntlets to offer a bare and vulnerable hand as a sign of friendship and as an act of faith. Today if you are wearing gloves and you are introduced to someone who is not, remove your gloves to shake hands. Knights and ladies removed their gloves when eating. Today as in the age of knights, remove gloves when eating.

* A Note for Men
Men remove gloves when shaking hands with women. The man may leave his gloves on without apologizing if it is too awkward and time consuming to remove his gloves. Men remove gloves when inside buildings unless the gloves are part of a wedding ensemble or dress for a fancy ball.

*A Note for Women
Long gloves are still worn at very formal dances in America and in other parts of the world. Women do not need to remove gloves when shaking hands. Gloves are

left on at dances, receptions and in receiving lines. The custom is to wear bracelets over and rings under gloves. Women remove gloves before eating, drinking, playing cards or applying makeup. Long, elbow-length gloves should be removed as soon as a lady is seated at a dining table. Gloves are never placed on the table or the arms of chairs. Women wearing gloves with buttons at the wrist who do not wish to remove them when dancing or drinking, may remove just the hand part and roll that part of the glove inward towards the wrist and tuck it under.

Glove wearing customs vary throughout the world. For example, in the northern parts of Europe, but not in the southern, it is the custom to shake hands with gloves on, off, or rolled back and to drink and dance with gloves rolled back or off. However, a universal custom is to remove gloves totally when dining or when being wed.

Today, common sense prevails over chivalry. If it's cold outside, leave your gloves on to shake hands. Formal gloves worn for fashion, especially long kid gloves that do not have buttons and are difficult to remove may be left on when shaking hands both here and abroad.

RITES OF PASSAGE

The celebration of special occasions with family and friends can be fun if you know what to expect as well as the behavior that is expected of you.

The events you are invited to attend may be religious, social or educational and provide the opportunity to celebrate in a formal fashion with family and special friends.

When a ceremony takes place in a church or synagogue that is not your own, be sure to take care with your clothing and appearance. While you may not understand the intricacies of the ceremony, be respectful and pay attention during the ceremony. If you don't know exactly what to do, simply watch those around you. Ask your friend in advance about any special requirements or customs you might observe and not understand.

If you are the honoree at any of these events, you have special duties, too. As the host or hostess at the celebration, you are responsible for the comfort of your guests. Greet them at the door and introduce them to your parents and other guests. Always write a prompt and sincere thank you note for all gifts received.

The First Communion

For a Roman Catholic child, the First Communion is commemorated at age seven when the child receives the sacrament for the first time during a special ceremony. The participants have attended special classes to learn about the significance of this event. Family and friends are usually invited back to the home for a special luncheon or party to celebrate this event. A white cake is traditionally served and the child receives gifts to commemorate this special occasion. An appropriate gift is a small book of prayers, stationery or small jewelry of a religious nature.

The Confirmation

Roman Catholics, Protestant and Reformed Jewish faiths have a Confirmation ceremony which signifies the maturation and coming of age of its young adults. The young persons attend classes to learn about the history, doctrines and beliefs of their church. During a formal ceremony the young adults confirm their faith and agree to live by the beliefs of their religion. Confirmands are often honored with a luncheon or reception that includes family and friends. A traditional white cake is served. Guests should bring an appropriate gift of a religious or symbolic nature to mark the occasion.

The Bat Mitzvah and Bar Mitzvah

Coming of age in the Jewish community is celebrated on the thirteenth birthday with a Bat Mitzvah for girls, and a Bar Mitzvah for boys. Again, the young persons have studied the Jewish religion for years and actively participate in the ceremony. The ceremony signifies the acceptance as an adult member of the congregation. Special parties are often held after the ceremony and may include dining and dancing. An appropriate gift is one that is long-lasting such as jewelry, a leather wallet or billfold, a book, personalized stationery or a nice pen and pencil set. Gifts from family may be more lavish and often include money.

Graduations

Graduations from high school and college are filled with excitement for the graduate. Most graduates are honored with a special dinner or party of close family and friends. Graduation gifts tend to be more lavish and are often gifts of money.

Weddings

Weddings are joyous events and are usually quite formal. Guests should wear their best clothes, but women should refrain from wearing white, in deference to the bride. During the religious ceremony, observe those around you if the church is not your own. At some churches, any Christian can partake of Holy Communion. Ask your friend or a parent to clarify such customs. A lavish reception normally follows the religious ceremony. There will usually be dining, dancing and socializing.

Sometimes there will be a receiving line after the ceremony or as you arrive at the reception. Most couples register their gift preferences at local stores. Choose your gift and send it in advance. Either have the store deliver it or take it to the bride's home in person. Gifts taken to the reception are often misplaced or stolen and sometimes the gift card disappears.

Funerals

A funeral is probably the most solemn event you will attend. While you may feel sad or uncomfortable, remember that you are present to express your sympathy to the family. You should always dress up for the visit to the funeral home or church. When you see the grieving family, simply say "I'm so sorry" or "Uncle Harry was very special to me." A condolence letter will also be appreciated.

GIFT-GIVING

The custom of giving gifts is present in every culture. A good idea is to explore the customs and traditions of other cultures if you have friends in other countries whose gift-giving traditions may be different from your own. This is not only thoughtful but may prevent considerable embarrassment. A few samples of international gift-giving customs follow as well as gift-giving guidelines in the United States.

International Gift-Giving Customs

In France and Italy, dinner guests traditionally send flowers before going to dinner at a friend's house. In Great Britain, flowers are generally sent after the dinner. Not only is it important to know when to send flowers but also how many and what kind. The French would be insulted if an odd number of flowers (7, 11, and 13) were sent! The color and type of flower sent also has meaning in certain countries. Red roses represent love; yellow roses suggest good bye or the end of a relationship. White flowers and long lasting chrysanthemums are the symbol of death in some cultures.

The Dutch and Scandinavians expect dinner and houseguests to bring presents. They also open the gifts in the presence of their guests and thank them immediately. The hostess gift is not essential to the French and the Thais.

Gift-giving etiquette in some countries requires that the gift be wrapped while in other countries it is not important. So wrap your box of chocolates to an Italian hostess but do not bother to wrap for your German host.

While flowers, food and special drinks are welcome gifts almost everywhere, there are some cultures which might be offended by your choice of gift. For instance, never take special drinks to a dinner with a Spaniard, Portuguese or Italian, as it would be as insulting as arriving with your own food. Look it up or ask when in doubt!

Gift-giving customs in Japan are more involved than the gift-giving customs in most countries. In Japan, a beautifully wrapped present is important as are the paper colored wrappings used. The gift should not be too expensive as a present of equal value is expected given to the giver by the recipient on the next occasion.The Japanese never open their presents in front of the giver for fear that their facial expressions might reflect some disappointment over the gift.

North American Gift-Giving Customs

In the United States, presents may be given at any time to hosts, close friends and family at Christmas, Chanukah, birthdays and special occasions. (See Rites of Passage) Consider the needs and feelings of others when selecting gifts for them. Guests who are invited to a dinner party or to be houseguests often remember the host with a gift. The hostess should try to open the gift in the presence of the giver and thank the giver at that time.

Avoid giving:

- High calorie presents to people who have weight problems

- Gifts which may not be appreciated and may place burdens on the receiver and other household members (i.e. animals, telephones, exotic equipment)

- Gifts that might make the receiver feel that you pity his/her situation (statements like "I noticed that you didn't have..." might make the receiver feel uncomfortable)

- Gift certificates or tokens which cannot be used in the area where the recipient resides

- Personal items or intimate apparel unless it is for a very close family member

"If you are late with a letter, don't apologize so much it makes it seem that having to write is just the final straw on top of everything else that's happened to you."

Sheila Ostrander

THANK YOU NOTES

People who do nice things for you appreciate knowing that you like what they have done for you. Saying "thank you" is one way to let them know that you are grateful, and in our modern times of electronic communication, e-mails and faxes are additional ways to send an instant message of appreciation. However, the personal touch of a handwritten note has yet to be replaced. The famous Crane ad is true, "To our knowledge no one has ever cherished a fax."

Writing a thank you note does not need to take a lot of time, but its impact can be great. The sooner you write the note, the less you'll need to write. The important thing to do is to write it. People will appreciate your written thanks whether you write the note in pencil on notebook paper or on fine vellum. Remember, good manners refers to the treatment of people the way you wish to be treated while etiquette refers to the written social rules which have evolved in a particular culture. American etiquette dictates the preferred color of ink as black and that special selections of paper be used for different types of correspondence.

General Good Manners for Writing a Thank You Note

Thank people for having you as a guest for a special meal, party, overnight visit, gift, or for anything they have done especially nice for you such as help you with a difficult project.

- Write and send your written note within a week after someone has done something special for you.

- Write your note on clean, nice paper.

- Use your best penmanship. Be neat.

- Use good grammar and look up the correct spelling of any words you do not know how to spell.

- Write your note as though you were talking to the person.

- Specify the kindness and tell why you appreciate it.

- Include a personal note about you and your family.

- Add something personal, funny, or nice.

- Try to avoid beginning your thank you note with "Thank you for…" For example, begin the note by saying something like "It was so much fun to be at your house Friday evening." "I appreciate you remembering me on my graduation."

Stationary to Use for Writing a Thank You Note

The hand-written note is a powerful tool in today's technological world. Receiving a hand-addressed letter on high-quality stationery is much more gratifying than a curled, faded, word-processed note that arrived via facsimile. Have a supply of note cards in your desk—it takes only a few minutes to write a quick note.

Everyone should have a box of plain, unpersonalized letter sheets. These are the appropriate papers for replying to formal invitations or writing condolence letters.

A vast array of social stationery is available today ranging from formal to casual in style. Following is a list of some of the types of stationery you may want to have as you correspond with family and friends.

Informal Folded Cards for Women

Informal folded cards, often incorrectly referred to as informals, are rather formal small note cards folded across the top. These notes are the smallest mailing size allowed by the US Postal Service. Women typically use these cards. Married couples may use them when issuing informal invitations. They may be engraved or printed with the woman's name, name of a married couple, or the woman's complete married name. Informal folded cards are frequently used for issuing or responding to invitations, sending brief notes, thank-you notes, or as gift enclosures. (Note that Crane Stationers advises that informal folded cards are not properly used as thank you notes or calling cards, and should never be used by single men.) They are either white or ecru and printed with black ink. Writing begins on the inside, below the note's fold. Keep your message brief and do not write on the back of the card. Place the informal folded card into its envelope bottom edges first with the print facing the envelope flap so that the name will be seen first when the card is removed from its envelope.

Notes for Women

Notes are identical to the informal folded cards but are printed with the woman's monogram or her name written in full. Notes are used for the same purposes as informal folded cards, and may be used for thank you notes. Writing can begin on page one (the front of the note) when the monogram or name is at the top of the note. Writing begins on page three (inside the note below the fold) when the monogram or name is centered on the front of the note.

Correspondence Cards for Men and Women

Correspondence cards are heavy weight cards marked with your name or monogram. They are available in plain ecru or white as well as bordered, and in a variety of colors. They range in style from very formal to casual and are used for brief notes, thank you notes, holiday greetings and birthday wishes. Writing should be on the front side only. Place the correspondence card into its envelope bottom edge first with the writing facing the envelope flap so it will be most easily seen when the card is removed from its envelope. Men use correspondence cards instead of notes.

Message Cards

Message cards are similar to correspondence cards except they bear the woman's complete social name and title (Miss, Mrs.) at the top center of the card. The address of the woman appears in the upper right-hand corner. Crane stationers decree that only the street address be printed here if the address is in a large city and that the street address, city, and state be printed when the address is a small town. The zip code is not included on the message card, but will correctly appear with the complete address of the sender on the envelope's back flap. The return address is printed on the back of envelopes used for social stationery although the US Postal Service prefers printing on the front of the envelope. The sender's name is not printed on the envelope of social stationery.

Half-Sheets for Men and Women

The half sheet is stationery paper that folds in half to fit in its envelope. Half sheets may be printed or engraved with a monogram, name and/or address. They are used for letters and thank you notes. Avoid writing on the back of the sheet and use a plain second sheet if you need room for a longer message. If you need room for a longer message, use a plain second sheet.

Women's Formal Letter Sheets

Folded letter sheets are the most formal of social stationery. Formal letter sheets have a folded edge down the left side and are folded again in half from top to bottom to fit an envelope half its size.

Formal letter sheets are ecru or white and can be printed with a name or monogram. These can be used for a variety of purposes including letters, thank you notes and issuing invitations. Plain unmarked formal letter sheets are the most correct stationery for a woman to use for issuing a wedding invitation or a letter of sympathy. Use black ink and begin writing on page one, then page three, and then page two if necessary. Write on the back of the sheet (page four) if necessary.

Men's Formal Social Writing Paper

Men use single sheets of good heavy quality paper that fits into a rectangular envelope when the sheet is folded once across the center. Black ink is used and writing does not continue onto the back of the sheet.

Calling Cards

Calling cards are believed to have originated in China when communication was conducted in one of two ways- by letter or face to face conversation. The custom of making social calls to the homes of friends was therefore very important. The calling card was designed for use by the visitor to leave behind at the residence of the person who was not at home at the time of the call. Today military personnel primarily use calling cards in the old way. A modern use for calling cards is as an enclosure or gift card by children and adults.

Envelopes

The return address is correctly placed on the center of the back flap of an envelope containing a social note. However, The US Postal Service prefers the return address be placed on the front of the envelope on the upper left-hand corner, but does not require it.

Start the address in the middle of the envelope. Write the name of the person the letter is to on the first line. Be sure to include the person's correct title. (see honorifics) On the second line, write the street address; and on the third line, write the city, state (which should be spelled out) and zip code. The city and state are separated with a comma.

Writing Instruments

Formal thank you notes are written with ink pens. Black ink is the preferred traditional color.

A Sample Thank You Note

Dear Dorothea,

The clock radio you gave me for my birthday is terrific. My old one would only get AM stations and had so much static that it was no fun to listen to. I hated waking up to that awful noise. Now when I wake up I hear pleasant sounds and I think of you. It's also great to be able to tune in to different stations during the day to match my different moods. I really appreciate your thoughtfulness.

How do you like your new job as Director of the North Carolina History Associates? We are thrilled that you accepted the position. You'll provide outstanding leadership.

Our family is fine. Win and Allison are counting the days until school is out. Gene is on the golf course every spare minute.

We hope to see you, Geff and the rest of your family at the beach soon. Thank you again for the clock radio.

Love,
Jane

FORMS OF ADDRESS and CORRESPONDENCE

Begin your letter with a salutation. Dear is the most popular word to use. If you are writing to a close friend simply write:

Dear Bill
Dear Allison

- Use an honorific such as Mr., Mrs., Dr., Miss or Ms. when you address someone in writing who is not a close friend or relative. For example:

Dear Mrs. Hight
Dear Ms. Wessell
Dear Mr. Williams

Dear Miss Cherry
Dear Dr. McMurry

- Use an honorific for everyone when addressing the envelope. For example:

Mrs. Henry Wesley Hight
Mr. Stephen Covington

Miss Virginia Taylor
Dr. Elias Albert Jones, Jr.

- Use the honorific Master when addressing an envelope to a young man aged 12 and under. Use Mr. after the age of 13. For example, Master Charles Boiskey (until age 12), Mr. Charles Boiskey (after the age 13)

- Use the honorific Miss when addressing an envelope to a young girl or woman. Use the honorific Mrs. when a woman marries. Use the honorific Ms. when a woman enters the business arena. Ms. is a neutral term that does not signify marital status. Look at the following examples:

Address a woman who is not married:
Miss Martha Jane Hight or Miss Hight

Address a woman who is married or widowed and never divorced:
Mrs. John Eugene McMurry, Jr. or Mrs. McMurry (a woman's social married name does not change upon husband's death)

Address a professional woman who may or may not be married:
Ms. Jane Hight McMurry or Ms. McMurry

- Use the honorific Mrs. with the woman's first name when addressing an envelope to a woman who is divorced. For example, a woman, Sarah Smith, who was married to Sam Smith, was socially known as Mrs. Sam Smith (Mrs. Smith), but upon her divorce she is correctly addressed in social correspondence as Mrs. Sarah Smith (Mrs. Smith).

- List the woman's name first, then the man's, then the names of children by age from oldest to youngest when signing a greeting card. For example, Jane, Gene, Winifred and Allison McMurry.

INVITATIONS
AND
THE APPROPRIATE RESPONSE

Invitations can range in formality from an engraved invitation for a wedding or black-tie event to an informal invitation for a wedding or black-tie event to an informal invitation or phone call. All invitations require a response and the form of the invitation dictates the type of response required. Respond to a telephoned invitation with a telephone call after you've checked your calendar, or in person if the invitation has been extended face to face. Respond to any invitation you receive quickly as the organizers of the event need to know how many persons to expect in order to plan adequately for food, dancing, party favors, etc.

Responding to Formal Invitations

A formal invitation is extended in the third person and will usually have the French words for "Respond if you please" *Repondez sil vous plait* or *R.s.v.p.* in the lower left-hand corner. These words are intended as a command and not as a suggestion. Failure to respond is extremely bad manners. Unless a response card is included with the invitation that simply requires the recipient to fill in a reply and mail back in the envelope provided, a formal invitation should be responded to on a formal, folded letter sheet. The response should be written in the third person, using the following formula:

Acceptance:

Miss Winifred Joan McMurry
accepts with pleasure
the kind invitation of
The Junior Charity League
Saturday, the sixth of June
from seven until nine in the evening
Cleveland County Country Club

Regret:

Master Winston Heath Hammond
regrets that he is unable
to accept the very kind invitation of
The Middleburg Hunt Club
to attend the Hunt Breakfast
Saturday, the tenth of November
Fox and Hound Club

Responding to Informal Invitations

Informal invitations may include the words "Regrets only" or "R.s.v.p." accompanied by a telephone number. The invitation containing "Regrets only" with the telephone number requires a telephoned response whether or not you plan to attend. The invitation containing "Regrets only" accompanied by the telephone number requires a response only if you are unable to attend. Respond to all invitations in a timely manner.

TELEPHONE SKILLS

Answering the Telephone

1. SAY: "Hello."
    The right way to answer a telephone in the home is to simply say "hello." It is not necessary to identify yourself or give your telephone number for security reasons. (Strangers often invade homes seeking information and offering to sell products to the occupants.) Wait for the caller to identify him/herself before supplying your name, telephone number, address or other information.

2. SAY: "This is (s) he" or "This is Win McMurry" if the call is for you.

3. SAY: "Please hold," or "Just a minute," when the caller asks to speak to someone in your home. If the call is for another member of the family, ask: "May I ask who's calling?" or "May I tell my mother who's calling?" not "Who is this?"

4. DO place the receiver on the table quietly without slamming it or letting it bang against the floor or wall when the call is for someone else. Take the telephone away from your mouth before calling in a medium-toned voice for the person. Inform the other household member of his/her call by walking into the room where the other household member is. Covering the telephone mouthpiece and yelling should be avoided. For example, in a medium toned

voice say, "Allison, you have a phone call." Do not yell, "Allison, a boy is on the phone for you!" or "Mom, it's that woman who talks too much on the phone for you!"

5. If the call is for a parent who isn't home, say, "My mother can't come to the phone right now. May I take a message?" not "My parents are away for the evening."

Making the Telephone Call

1. Identify yourself and state your purpose.
   SAY: "Hello, this is Allison McMurry. May I please speak to Thomas?" Not "Is Thomas there?" When Thomas does answer your call, do ask if it is a convenient time to talk. If it is not, find out when you should call back.

   If the person you're calling isn't available, don't just hang up! It is correct to ask if the person will take a message such as, "Will you please tell him I called? I'm wondering if he can go to the play tonight. Will you ask him to call me back?" Don't ask nosy questions such as, "Where is he?" "Is he at Georgia's house?"

2. DO speak clearly. Avoid eating while talking.

3. DO keep the background noise in your home quiet. Loud radios and televisions can make conversations difficult.

4. DO focus your attention on the person to whom you are speaking. Speaking to others in the room with you should be avoided.

5. DO call between 9 a.m. and 9 p.m. Most families don't like to be disturbed during dinner or after 9:00 p.m. in the evening. Be considerate! If you are calling between 5:00 and 7:00 ask "Am I disturbing your dinner?" Calling before 9:00 a.m. on a weekend is not a good idea either.

6. DO keep calls brief. Telephone calls should rarely be longer that ten minutes. Remember that others may need to use the telephone line or have other things to do. Ask if it is a convenient time to talk. "Is this a good time to talk?" or "Am I interrupting you?" "Do you have a minute to give me directions to the ski slopes?"

7. Remember that it is the caller's responsibility to end the call.

Call Waiting

1. DO wait until a break in conversation before responding to the call waiting signal. Courtesy to the first person you are on line with comes first. Then excuse yourself and say, "Please excuse me just a moment."

2. Switch to the second caller, say "Hello" and wait for the caller to identify her/himself.

3. If the call is for you, let the caller know immediately that you have someone on the other line and that you'll return the call in a few minutes. Then do so.

4. If the call is for another person, give the message as soon as possible.

5. If the call is for a parent or if the call is urgent and for another person, ask the second caller to hold and tell the first caller that you'll call them back later. DO SO. Immediately summon the person for whom the urgent call was made.

Answering Machines

1. The out-going message on your machine should be brief. Few people have time to listen to a lengthy message. Ten to fifteen seconds is an appropriate length.

2. Include a simple greeting such as "Hello" and then ask the caller to leave a message. A good sample message is: "Hello, please leave your name, telephone number, and message. Your call will be returned as soon as possible."

3. Providing your name and telephone number may give information to strangers which you may later regret.

4. Answering machines are now familiar to most callers. It is no longer necessary to include usage instructions such as "after the beep."

Leaving a Message on Someone Else's Machine

1. State your name, telephone number and the purpose of your call.

2. Remember that what you say on a machine may be heard by many people. Avoid leaving a message that might embarrass you or others.

3. Keep your message brief. The following is an example of a good message that is brief and includes essential information. "Hello, this is Win McMurry calling for Stephen Covington. It's 10:30 Saturday morning. I have tickets to the UNC basketball game tonight and wonder if you'd like to go with my sister and me. Please call me. Thank you. Bye."

How to Handle a Wrong Number

If you incorrectly dial a number say, "I'm sorry, I must have the wrong number."

If someone calls your number by mistake say, "I'm sorry, there is no one here by that name."

When the caller asks, "What number is this?" or "What residence is this?" reply, "What number are you trying to call? ... No, that's not our number." or "What number are you trying to call? ... No, you must have the wrong number." Never tell a stranger your name or phone number.

How to Take a Message

Have a pad of paper and a pencil by the phone. Ask for the name of the caller and his phone number. Ask the person to spell her name if you don't know how. Carefully write the phone number and repeat it—"Let me repeat the number, 438-5168?" Leave the message in an agreed-upon place—don't forget to let the person you took the message for know there was a call!

The following is an example of a good written message.

Dad, Dr. Fulk called at 8 p.m. Call him before midnight at 672-1854.

How to Handle a Prank Call

In today's world of caller ID and callback services, making prank telephone calls is not a smart idea. Chances are the culprit will be caught. Most importantly, prank calls are not kind and they make others uncomfortable. If you receive such a call, simply hang up. Don't scream or panic—that's just the response the person making the call wants. Always tell an adult when you receive a prank call. If the calls persist, contact the telephone company.

How to Handle Obscene Calls

If you receive an obscene or threatening phone call, immediately hang up on the caller. Then call the police. In some areas you may dial *57 for touch tone phones or 1157 for rotary phones to trace the call. (The charge for each trace is $3.45. Ask your telephone service provider to report the calls to police (requires $5 processing fee) after two successful traces within a 30-day period. If call trace is not available in your area, call your telephone service provider's annoyance call bureau at 800-640-2043.)

SPORTSMANSHIP

Most of us will participate in sports activities throughout our lives. Not only do sports provide physical exercise, they teach us to work together as a team and help us develop self-confidence. They also provide a social outlet for both children and adults. Sports etiquette is not always spelled in the rules, but it should be understood and practiced if a player wants to be known as sportsmanlike.

We've all witnessed unbecoming behaviors during sporting events. Not everyone can be the best or be the winner all the time. But you'll enjoy yourself and will be a valuable asset to your team if you remember the points listed below.

1. Remember, there is no "I" in TEAM. Do your part by learning the rules of every game you play so you can play fair.

2. Never give up.

3. Practice self-discipline. Control your temper. Assume responsibility and don't blame others.

4. Be loyal to your team. Encourage teammates always.

5. Lead by example.

6. Respect your opponent. Remember they work as hard as you do to succeed. Good sports do not do anything to distract people from playing the game.

7. Be a gracious winner and a gracious loser. Both are short-lived. Good sports do not complain about the rules, the coach or the referee. Good losers do not make excuses for their performance or the performance of their teammates. Compliment the winner on his performance after a game. When you are the winner, console the loser on his loss, but not on his performance.

8. Take care of your body. Practice good nutrition so you'll feel up to the challenge.

9. Welcome challenges with enthusiasm.

10. Welcome constructive criticism. Be able to take it as well as you give it.

11. Be willing to give more than you take.

12. See opportunity in every difficulty.

13. Smile - a gentle curve which straightens many things.

14. Be committed to your goals. Visualize them always.

DANCE ETIQUETTE

Dancing is a skill you can learn. Take lessons so you can enjoy its primary purpose which is to enjoy the companionship of others and to have fun moving together to the beat of music. This fun activity has a few rules which knowing will make you feel confident on the dance floor.

First, let's talk about a few of the manners to remember when you are attending dancing classes.

When you enter the ballroom for your classes you may be asked to enter in what is called escort position. You have probably observed this when attending weddings where groomsmen escorted women to their seats.

Escort Position

The man bends his right arm at the elbow and makes a fist, placing the fist right below the rib cage. He should stand very straight and tall. His partner should place her fingertips lightly on his forearm. She does not grab his arm tightly or use him as total support. The couple greets the instructor before the session begins. The teacher of the class may assign you a partner or you may be given an opportunity to ask someone to dance.

How to Ask a Partner to Dance

The young man walks up to the woman of his choice. He DOES NOT scrutinize each young woman at the dance before making his decision. If he does not know the girl, he introduces himself to her and asks if she would care to dance, "May I have this dance?" If the girl does not know him, she introduces herself. The girl accepts the dance by saying, "Yes, thank you." If the girl is standing, the boy offers her his arm and escorts her onto the dance floor. If she is seated, he should extend his left hand, palm up. She accepts his hand with her right hand palm facing down and he gently helps her rise. Again, he offers her his right arm and escorts her onto the dance floor.

When the song has ended, the young man escorts the young woman back to her seat. He seats her properly if she was sitting previously. He thanks her for the dance and she reciprocates with a thank you.

Points to Remember

A dance is just a dance—not a commitment for life! If someone asks you to dance it is a compliment. Accept if at all possible. It takes courage to ask someone to dance and no one likes rejection. After all, a dance usually doesn't last more than three to five minutes. The traditional way to ask someone to dance is to say, "May I  have this dance?" The traditional reply is "I'll be delighted" or if she has already accepted the dance with someone else, "I'm so sorry, this one is taken."

Never decline a dance with a false excuse and then accept when someone you like better comes along. That will hurt the feelings of the first person. If you tell someone you are going for refreshments or to the rest room, go!

Never roll your eyes or laugh when someone asks you to dance. Always be considerate of the other person's feelings.

If you aren't comfortable with the dance steps, be honest with your partner. Perhaps he or she can help you. Say, "Excuse me" if you do step on your partner's feet.

It is perfectly acceptable for girls to ask boys to dance, too!

After dancing with a girl, it is polite for the man to say to his partner, "Thank you." The polite response from the woman is "I enjoyed it too" or something else such as "It was fun" or "It was a pleasure." However, girls do not traditionally thank men for a dance.

Formal Dances

A gentleman who invites a lady to a dance is expected to send her flowers on the day of the dance. Some men prefer to present the flower to the woman when they call for her. The flowers may be a small bouquet or a corsage which may be worn by the woman on her dress or wrist.

It is good manners for him to telephone her ahead of time to find out what she is wearing so he can order flowers that will complement her outfit. (Flowers are not expected to be sent before a simple, informal dance.) The woman is expected to wear the flower either on her dress, wrist, or purse. It is appropriate for the woman to present the man with a boutonniere (a small flower worn in the man's lapel), when he arrives to pick her up for the dance.

A man who drives to pick up his date should get out of his car and walk to the woman's door. Never blow your horn or ask her to wait outside for you when you plan to pick her up! Greet her family, help her with her coat if she has one, walk with her to the car, open the car door for her and help her in and out of the car. At the end of the evening, help her in and out of the car and walk her to her door.

The first responsibility of guests at every dance or party after they have checked their coats is to go together to find the host and hostess of the party and greet them. At the end of the party, guests should find their hosts again and thank them for the party. The "plus one" rule is to add one special comment about the evening to the thank you. Greeting hosts at the beginning of the party and saying thank you before leaving the party are important courtesies that should never be overlooked.

The man who has asked a woman to a dance should always dance the first dance with the woman he invited to the party. He may dance with other women at the party so long as the woman he has invited has a partner. If the man's partner is invited to dance with another man, he may choose to find a partner or "cut in" on a couple who is dancing.

Cutting In

Men "cut in" by tapping the arm of the girl's partner. The man being tapped should step aside and allow the man cutting in to dance with his partner. When the person being tapped is dancing with the girl for the first time during the evening, he may smile and say "Next time around." If he does this, he must allow the man trying to cut in to dance with his partner the next dance. The girl always says, "I'm sorry" or something similar when leaving one partner for another partner. It is good manners for her not to show preference for one man over another as they have each paid her a compliment by asking her to dance.

Male guests at a party should try to dance with the hostess of a party.

Have fun!

"Don't make a wall around your plate with your left arm as if you feared somebody were going to snatch it from you."

Gloria Goddard

DINING SKILLS

Whether you are eating at home, in a fast food or fancy restaurant, table manners are important. No one wants to share a meal with a person who is gross to look at while eating and behaves crudely. Wherever you eat make sure you wash your hands before eating.

Seating

It is polite for children and men to wait for women to take their seats (offer to assist with seating) before

they sit. A man accompanying a woman to dinner helps to

seat her. He does this by holding the top of the chair with both hands and pulling the chair out from the table. The woman enters the chair from the right side, sits on the edge and places her hands on the side of the chair. The man gently pushes the chair forward

while the woman adjusts her seat. The man enters his chair from the right and seats himself so that the woman is seated on his right.

Sit in the chair with comfortable straight posture. Lean slightly forward when eating. Arms and elbows should not be on the table when food is on the table. It is acceptable to place elbows on the table when no food is on the table and you are in a noisy restaurant and must lean forward to be heard by your dining companions.

Avoid tipping your chair back as you may fall as well as break the furniture!

American style dining requires that hands remain in the lap except when using silverware. European style dining requires that the hands stay at table level with the wrists touching the table's edge except when lifting food to the mouth.

Remember to push your chair up to the table and sit up straight. Lift your food - a hamburger or filet mignon - to your mouth without hovering over your plate. Place your napkin on your lap unless you are under five years of age or eating lobster. Wait for everyone to be served and for the host to begin before you start to eat. Use the silver ware farthest from your plate first when you are faced with lots of utensils.

The man sits opposite the woman or to the left of her. It is courteous for the man to offer the woman the most comfortable seat and the seat with the best view. At tables scattered throughout the restaurant, women sit across from each other. Women sit nearest the wall when seated at booths or tables positioned

near the wall. A man may sit across from the woman when they are alone, but it is traditionally correct for him to sit beside her.

The Blessing

The custom of saying grace or giving thanks for food generally precedes the meal in the United States. Some people choose to stand for the blessing, others remain seated for the blessing, while others may choose to hold hands while giving thanks. Guests should follow the lead of their hosts. A guest who does not share the same faith is not expected to participate in this religious moment. However, the good guest will show respect by remaining still and silent at this time. In public places, most diners give thanks silently especially when they are part of a group of diners of mixed religions. A family dining out together may correctly choose to express thanks aloud.

Napkins

After age five, place your napkin in your lap and not around your neck after the hostess places hers in her lap. Pick the napkin up by its corner with the left hand and place it in your lap with the fold to your waist. Smaller luncheon napkins are completely unfolded and placed in the lap. If you must leave the table during the meal (only for an emergency) place your napkin in your seat. This indicates to the waiter that you will return to your seat and that you are not finished. Pick your napkin up from the center and place it to the left of your plate when you have finished dinner. Wait for your hostess to do this first.

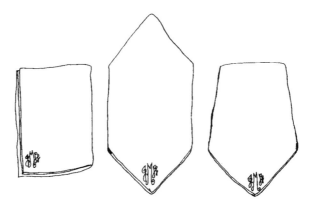

Napkins may be folded in a variety of ways. The fold of the napkin on the left is the most formal. It is also the simplest. The napkin on the left is folded so that the fold is to the plate.

The Simple Place Setting

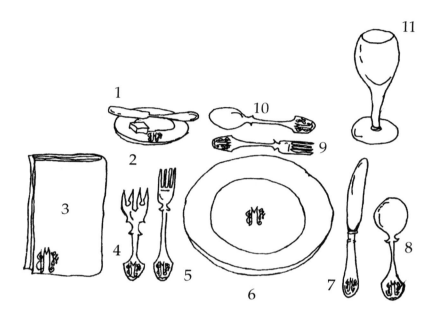

1. Butter Spreader
2. Bread and Butter Plate
3. Napkin
4. Salad Fork
5. Dinner Fork
6. Dinner Plate

7. Dinner Knife
8. Soup Spoon
9. Dessert Fork
10. Dessert Spoon
11. Water Goblet

How to Hold Flatware

Try this trick to get the idea of how to correctly hold flatware for cutting food. Place the knife in your right hand and the fork in your left hand. Balance the handle of the knife and fork on your index fingers. Now, gently grasp the handles and turn the knife and fork over facing the plate. The index finger of your right hand should be pointing down the blade of the knife and the index finger of the left hand pointing down towards the tines of the fork.

Correct American style requires that after a bite of food is cut, the knife be placed at the top of the plate with the blade facing the diner. The fork is then transferred to the right hand where it is held with the thumb and index finger about half way up the handle. The middle finger supports the fork while the rest of the fingers gently grasp the handle. The spoon is held in the same fashion.

Eating Etiquette

Do not begin to eat until everyone has been served. Wait for the hostess to lift her fork before you begin. Chew food with your mouth closed and keep your arms close to your body when you eat. If you are seated at a long banquet table where many people are eating, you may begin when those around you have been served.

- Use the silverware farthest from the plate for your first course and work your way in as the meal progresses when enjoying a set menu offered for everyone. The table has been set with that menu in mind. (When in doubt, follow your host's lead) At restaurants, the table is set not knowing what individuals will order. Learn the placement of items so you'll know the intended use of each utensil and the placement of your bread and butter plate.

• Cut food one bite at a time.

• Cut food into bite-sized pieces.

• Put down your knife and fork between bites when eating in the American style.

• Hold your knife and fork between bites with tines and blades parallel to your plate, or cross your silverware and place it on the plate when eating in the European (Continental) dining style.

How to Eat Soup

Spoon the soup away from you. It is correct to tilt the soup plate slightly away from you if necessary to get the soup in the spoon. Sip soup from the side of the spoon. Never put the entire bowl of the spoon into your mouth.

The spoon should rest on the right side of the saucer under the consommé cup or cream soup bowl. Never leave your spoon standing in these shallow dishes. The soup plate is larger and can accommodate a spoon resting on its surface.

*"Blow not your broth at table but stay till it
cools of itself."*

George Washington

*Whenever you are eating soup
Remember not to be a Goop!
And if you think to say this rhyme,
Perhaps 'twill help you every time:*

*Like little boats that put to sea,
I push my spoon AWAY from me;
I do not tilt my dish nor scrape
The last few drops like hungry ape!*

*Like little boats, that, almost filled,
Come back without their cargoes spilled,
My spoon sails gently to my lips,
Unloading from the SIDE, like ships.*

Gellett Burgess

RESTAURANT SAVVY

Dining in a restaurant is a treat. No one in your family has to set the table or load the dishwasher. Eating in a restaurant is a great opportunity to visit with your family and eat different kinds of food that may not be served at home.

Some restaurants are casual and serve the kinds of food with which we are familiar - hot dogs, hamburgers and pizza are always favorites! Ethnic restaurants serve food familiar to a particular country - Chinese, Indian, Mexican, Italian and Lebanese, to name a few. Specialty restaurants serve certain types of food as well - such as seafood or pizza.

Some restaurants are formal. There may be fancy starched linens and more flatware than you usually see at home. The people dining may be more dressed up and the atmosphere may be more quiet and reserved.

Restaurant Manners to Remember:

- Dress appropriately. Remember, neat and clean are always in style. At a fast-food restaurant almost any kind of clothing goes. At nice, casual restaurants sweats or exercise clothes are not a good choice - but clean jeans and a tucked-in shirt might be okay. At formal restaurants jeans are not a good choice - men should wear khaki or corduroy pants and a shirt with a collar (and even perhaps a jacket and tie!) Women should wear a skirt and blouse or sweater or a dress.

- Wait quietly to be seated.

- Remain in your seat after you are seated. It's okay to smile and say hello if you see a friend—but do not visit his table. Visiting a table requires that the family members stop eating to talk. Standing by someone's table also creates an obstruction for the wait staff. If you need to visit the rest room, ask to be excused. Unless you are ill, one visit is all you should make.

- Don't touch anything on the table until the host/hostess picks up her napkin.

- Don't play with the flatware, the candle, the sugar packets or salt and pepper shakers.

- Look at the menu carefully and choose food you will enjoy eating. Ask your host for suggestions if you are not familiar with the food. Asking for a recommendation from your host also gives you an idea of the price range your host probably wants you to observe. When ordering, look at the server so he will clearly understand you.

- Keep the noise level at your table to a minimum. People sitting at other tables shouldn't be able to hear your conversation.

- Turn to the waiter, look him in the eye, and clearly give your order. Smile. Say, 'May I please have the chicken supreme." Not "I want the chicken thing."

- Don't eat too much bread or too many appetizers. Eat your bread by tearing off one bite at a time. Butter each bite. Save room for your meal.

- Say "please" when you ask for something and "thank-you" when the waiter or someone serves you food or passes you something. Keep your conversation with the waiter to a minimum. They are working and a prolonged conversation prevents them from serving you and other guests efficiently.

- Move slightly to the right as the waiter places your food in front of you. He will serve your food to your left and remove your food from the right. Your beverages will be served and removed from the right.

- Sit up straight and properly in the chair with your feet in front of you. Dangling legs and chairs that are not pushed in properly can cause a waiter or another diner to trip and fall.

Finger Foods

Some foods are perfect for eating with your hands. Foods that have a "handle" such as shrimp and firm asparagus may also be picked up with your fingers.

- Pizza
- Sandwiches without gravy
- Hamburgers
- Hot-Dogs
- Tortillas
- Artichokes
- Grapes
- Corn on the Cob
- Olives

Sometime Finger Foods

- Bacon when it is crisp

- Bananas when you are alone, but if it is sliced, eat it with a spoon or fruit fork

- French-fries

- Fried chicken at picnics

- Watermelon when it is not served with utensils - usually outside or at a picnic

- Apples when you are alone or on a picnic. Cut and quarter apples in a restaurant.

- Celery. Eat it by hand. If you like salt, place some on your plate and dip the celery into it.

How to Eat Apples and Pears

Quarter apples and pears with a knife, peel the skin off if you choose, core, and eat with your fingers.

How to Eat Grapes and Cherries

Eat grapes and cherries whole using your hand. Note: break off a branch of grapes--not single grapes when you serve yourself from a fruit tray. Sometimes grape shears are placed beside the fruit tray for this purpose.

How to Eat Peaches, Plums, and Nectarines

Eat these fruits with your hands by first cutting the fruit in half, removing the stone, and finally, if you choose, removing the skin.

How to Eat Oranges

Peel oranges with the fruit knife and eat by sections or by half sections if the sections are large.

How to Eat Bananas

Bananas eaten at the table are completely peeled, placed on a plate, and cut into pieces or sliced and eaten with a fork. You may choose to place the banana on a plate, cut off both ends, and then with a fork and a knife, peel away the skin on a single bite-sized slice and eat it with a fork. Repeat. Save the monkey style for outdoor picnics and the hiking trail.

How to Eat Berries

Strawberries are the only berries not properly eaten solely with a spoon. Strawberries served with the hull are held by the stem and may be dipped in powdered sugar (from your plate, not the sugar dish) and eaten in a bite. Stems and hulls are placed on your plate.

Ten Tacky Table Offenders

Diners in a group often offend others at the table simply because they cannot see themselves as others can. Be aware that you unknowingly may have some personal habits that are repulsive. The top ten table offenses are listed.

1. Chewing food with an open mouth and forming it into a ball in one cheek. Chew small bites and do not chase your food with a beverage.

2. Talking with food in the mouth.

3. Making noise while eating such as smacking food, making cooing umm...umm...sounds and crunching ice. Eat and chew as quietly as possible. Not only is the sound of crunching ice annoying, it can also crack your teeth.

4. Blowing the nose, coughing or sneezing at the table without covering the mouth. (Excuse yourself from the table if you have time. If not, be sure to turn your head away from the table. Use a handkerchief, not the napkin.)

5. Asking for food without saying please and thank you.

6. Scratching and adjusting clothing at the table.

7. Talking about unappetizing or emotionally charged topics at the table.

8. Reaching across the table for food. Reach only for food that is within your personal space.

9. Gesturing with silverware.

10. Sopping food and pushing the plate away when finished.

Problems at the Table

Question: What do you do if you need your waiter and he is not available or is ignoring you?

Answer: You may stop another waiter or raise your hand slightly to get the attention of a waiter. Ask this waiter to send your waiter to you. Summon your waiter when he is in your vicinity by saying "Waiter" just loud enough for him to hear you if he is ignoring you. However, you should never yell out to your waiter in a restaurant, snap your fingers, or tap the table with your silverware to get his attention.

Question: What do you do if you drop your napkin or your silverware on the floor?

Answer: Leave the napkin or silverware on the floor so your waiter can see it. Let your waiter know that you need a clean napkin or silverware if he does not see it.

Question: What do you do if your china or silverware is not clean or if you see something on your place setting that is disagreeable?

Answer: Ask your waiter for a replacement. Do not draw unnecessary attention to the offending problem as it will interfere with others enjoyment of the meal.

What to Do When You Don't Like the Looks of Your Food

• Try a small bite. Even if it doesn't look the way your mama makes it, you may be pleasantly surprised. If you don't like it, don't make a big deal out of it. Saying loudly "Yuck! This is terrible!" is an insult to the chef.

• Tell the waiter if you especially like your meal. He will tell the chef. Everyone likes to be complimented!

Tipping

Good service is rewarded by the custom of tipping. Wait staff typically serve food, drinks, and answer menu questions. Wait staff in the United States are paid an amount lower than minimum wage so they expect tips of fifteen to twenty percent of the bill before taxes. A captain sometimes takes orders but does not serve. Captains expect a tip of five percent.

CONCLUSION

Life requires respiration. Taking in and giving out. If you have participated in my programs, read my books and now practice *The Dance Steps of Life*™ by giving of yourself, you'll find that you get back more than you give. You'll enjoy living like you've never enjoyed it before.

It is my hope that the formal rules, the etiquette, you learned will help you feel self-assured so that you can reach out to others and make them feel at ease for real happiness comes from not focusing on yourself but from thinking of others.

The aim of *The Etiquette Advantage*® programs is to make learning social skills interesting and fun. I have enjoyed watching participants bring valuable lessons to life through their participation in skits, role-plays, and other activities. It is a privilege to teach. I hope the participants have enjoyed our time together as much as I have.

In closing, I'd like to share with you research that shows that in order for a skill to become a habit, it must be consistently practiced for twenty-one days or it will be forgotten. Use this book to remember what you have learned for lack of these skills even on the smallest level can damage your image and hinder you as you try to achieve social and career goals. Practice *The Etiquette Advantage*® life lessons you've learned until they are a part of your everyday storehouse of skills. Good manners won't guarantee you a spot in the college or club of your choice, membership in your favorite fraternity or sorority, or later a seat in the executive boardroom, but without good manners the doors to those rooms will be closed to you forever. Practice.

Good luck as you use *The Dance Steps of Life*™ to become *Socially Smart*™ and make your dreams come true. May comfortable communication with others be yours and may you feel secure enough to have fun with many communication partners as you throw back your head and let your heart dance for the sheer joy of it!

Jane Hight McMurry

BIBLIOGRAPHY

Ailes, Roger. *You Are the Message*. New York: Doubleday, 1989.

Baldridge, Letitia. *More Than Manners*. New York: Rawson Associates, 1997.

Ballare, Antonia and Angelique Lanmpros. *Behavior Smart!* West Nyack, New York: The Center for Applied Research in Education, 1994.

Basic Social Skills For Youth. Boys Town, Nebraska: The Boys Town Press, 1992.

Begun, Ruth Weltmann, Editor. *Social Skills Lessons & Activities*. West Nyack, New York: Prentice Hall, 1996. (series for pre-k through grade 12)

Beyfus, Drusilla. *Parties: The Done Thing*. London: Ebury Press, 1992.

Bolton, Robert. *People Skills*. New York: Simon & Schuster, 1979.

Bowman, Daria Price and Maureen LaMarca. *Writing Notes With A Personal Touch*. New York; Michael Friedman Publishing Group, 1998.

Brant, Madeline. *The Etiquette of Dress*. Sussex, England: Copper Beech Publishing Ltd., 1996.

Bremer, Moyra. *Modern Etiquette and Successful Behaviour.* Oxford, England: Helicon Publishing, 1992.

Business and Social Etiquette with Disabled People. Springfield: Charles C. Thomas Publisher.

Donald, Elsie Burch. *Debrett's Etiquette of Modern Manners.* London: Pan Books Ltd., 1981.

Dowd, Tom and Jeff Tierney. *Teaching Social Skills to Youth.* Boys Town, Nebraska: The Boys Town Press, 1992.

Duvall, Lynn. *Respecting Our Differences.* Minneapolis: Free Spirit Publishing, Inc., 1994.

Duvall, Richard. *Character & Community.* Cypress, California: Creative Teaching Press, 1997.

Ephron, Delia and Edward Koren. *Do I Have To Say Hello?* New York: Viking Penguin, 1989.

Eyre, Lina and Richard. *Teaching Your Children Joy.* New York: Simon & Schuster, 1994.

Feinberg, Steven. *Crane's Blue Book of Stationery.* New York: Doubleday, 1989.

Fischer-Mirkin, Toby. *Dress Code.* New York: Clarkson Potter/Publishers, 1995.

Freeman, Sara. *Character Education.* Grand Rapids, Michigan: Instructional Fair, 1997.

Goodwin, Gabrielle and David Macfarlane. *Writing Thank-You Notes.* New York: Sterling Publishing Co., Inc., 1999.

Isaacs, Florence. *Just A Note To Say.* New York: Clarkson Potter/Publishers, 1995.

Johns, Allison Fuller. *Kids, Customs and Cultures.* Grand Rapids, Michigan: Instructional Fair.

Karns, Michelle. *How to Create Positive Relationships with Students.* Champaign, Illinois: Research Press, 1994.

Keller, Kate Van Winkler. *"If the Company can do it!"* Sandy Hook, Connecticut: The Hendrickson Group,1991.

Larkin, Jack. *The Reshaping of Everyday Life.* New York: Harper & Row, 1988.

Leaf, Munro. *Manners Can Be Fun.* New York: Harper & Row, Publishers, 1985.

Levine, Michael. *Raise Your Social I.Q.* Seacaucus, New Jersey: Carol Publishing Group, 1998.

Lindenfield, Gael. *Confident Children.* Hammersmith, London: Thorsons, 1994.

Long, Sheila. *Never Drink Coffee from Your Saucer.* Kansas City, Missouri: Andrews and McMeel, 1996.

McCullough, Donald. *Say Please, Say Thank You.* New York: G.P. Putnam's Sons, 1998.

Mole, John. *Mind Your Manners*. London: Nicholas Brealey Publishing Limited, 1996.

Morgan, John. *Debrett's New Guide To Etiquette & Modern Manners*. London: Headline Book Publishing, 1996.

Morganett, Rosemarie S. *Skills for Living*. Champaign, Illinois: Research Press, 1990.

Mosley, Charles. *Debrett's Guide To Entertaining*. London: Headline Book Publishing, 1994.

Myers, Elizabeth. *The Social Letter*. New York: The University Press, 1918.

Nish, Steven Nish, ed. *Good Ideas to Help Young People Develop Good Character*. Marina Del Ray, California: Josephson Institute, 1998.

Nix, William H. *Character Works*. Nashville, Tennessee: Broadman & Holman Publishers, 1999.

Orlick, Terry. *The Cooperative Sports & Games Book*. New York: Pantheon Books, 1978.

Osterberg, Richard. *Sterling Silver Flatware*. Schiffer Publishing Ltd., Atglen, Pennsylvania, 1994.

Panati, Charles. *Panati's Extraordinary Origins of Everyday Things*. New York: Harper & Rowe, 1989.

Paston-Williams, Sara. *The Art of Dining*. London: National Trust Enterprises Limited, 1993.

Pierce, Beatrice. *It's More Fun When You Know the Rules.* New York: Rinehart & Company, Inc., 1935.

Pincus, Debbie and Richard J. Ward. *Citizenship.* Carthage, Illinois: Good Apple, 1991.

Pincus, Debbie. *Manners Matter.* Parsippany, NJ: Good Apple, 1992.

Post, Elizabeth L. *Advice For Every Dining Occasion.* New York: Harper Collins Publishers, 1994.

Post, Elizabeth L. and Joan M. Coles. *Emily Post's Teen Etiquette.* New York: Harper Perennial, 1995.

Post, Emily. *Emily Post on Invitations and Letters.* New York: Harper & Row Publishers, 1990.

Post, Peggy. *Emily Post's Entertaining.* New York: Harper Collins, 1998.

Prichard, Mari. *Guests & Hosts.* Oxford, England: Oxford University Press, 1981.

Reekie, Jennie. *The London Ritz Book of Etiquette.* New York: William Morrow and Company, Inc., 1991.

Roberts, Patricia Easterbrook. *Table Settings, Entertaining, and Etiquette.* New York: Viking Press, 1967.

Roosevelt, Eleanor. *Eleanor Roosevelt's Book of Common Sense Etiquette.* New York: The Macmillan Company, 1962.

Ross, Pat. *The Pleasure of Your Company.* New York. Penguin Group, 1989.

Ross, Pat. *With Thanks & Appreciation*. New York: Viking Studio Books, 1989.

Sarnoff, Dorothy. *Never Be Nervous Again*. New York: Ivy Books, 1987.

Stewart, Marjabelle Young and Ann Buchwald. *Stand Up, Shake Hands, Say "How Do you Do."* New York: David McKay Company, 1977.

The Etiquette of Politeness. Sussex, England: Copper Beech Publishing Ltd., 1995.

Tiffany's Table Manners for Teenagers. New York: Random House, 1989.

Tuleja, Tad. *Curious Customs*. New York: Harmony Books, 1987.

Visser, Margaret. *The Rituals of Dinner*. New York: Grove Weidenfeld, 1991.

Vogue's Book of Etiquette and Good Manners. New York: The Conde Nast Publications, Inc., 1969.

Vogue's Book of Etiquette. Greenwich, Connecticut: The Conde Nast Publications, 1923.

Von Furstenberg, Diane. *The Table*. New York: Random House, 1996.

Washington, George. *Washington's Rules of Civility & Decent Behaviour In Company and Conversation*. Old Saybrook, Connecticut: Applewood Books, 1988.

Westmoreland, Rose. *Building Self-Esteem*. Torrance, California: Frank Schaffer Publication, Inc., 1994.

INDEX

ABOUT THE AUTHOR

Jane Hight McMurry

Socially Smart™ speaker, author, and trainer Jane Hight McMurry is the president of *Socially Smart*™and founder and managing director of **The Etiquette Advantage**® which provide training and support resources to help people achieve *Socially Smart*™ skills in communicating with people for professional and personal success. She is the author of *The Dance Steps of Life*™, *The Etiquette Advantage*®, *Readers Theatre for Senior Citizens*, and co-author of *Success is a Team Effort*. Jane speaks to audiences at all levels, from the frontline to the boardroom who want to achieve excellence in communicating with people.

Visit www.SociallySmart.com or telephone 910.762.0703 for more information about Jane Hight McMurry and the services of *Socially Smart*™ *and The Etiquette Advantage*®.

Quick Order Form

Please send the following books by Jane Hight McMurry.

QTY	ITEM	EACH	TOTAL
_____	*The Dance Steps of Life*™	$14.95	$_____
_____	*Success is a Team Effort*	$20.00	$_____
_____	*The Etiquette Advantage*®	$14.95	$_____
	SUBTOTAL		$_____

NC RESIDENTS ADD 6.5% SALES TAX $_____

POSTAGE AND HANDLING:
Add $2.00 one book + $ .90 more for each additional book.
CANADA: US Currency. ADD $3.00 for one book + $1.00
more for each additional book.

AMOUNT ENCLOSED $_____

<u>**FAX ORDER TO:**</u> 910-762-1766

<u>**MAIL ORDER TO:**</u>
Book Requests
PO Box 4544
Wilmington, NC 28406

<u>**SEND MY ORDER TO:**</u>

Name:

Address:

City: State: Zip:

Quick Order Form

Please send the following books by Jane Hight McMurry.

QTY	ITEM	EACH	TOTAL
_____	*The Dance Steps of Life*™	$14.95	$_____
_____	*Success is a Team Effort*	$20.00	$_____
_____	*The Etiquette Advantage*®	$14.95	$_____
	SUBTOTAL		$_____
NC RESIDENTS ADD 6.5% SALES TAX			$_____

POSTAGE AND HANDLING:
Add $2.00 one book + $ .90 more for each additional book.
CANADA: US Currency. ADD $3.00 for one book + $1.00
more for each additional book.

AMOUNT ENCLOSED $_____

FAX ORDER TO: 910-762-1766

MAIL ORDER TO:
Book Requests
PO Box 4544
Wilmington, NC 28406

SEND MY ORDER TO:

Name:

Address:

City: State: Zip